Glyn Hughes' YORKSHIRE

Millstone Grit Revisited

Photographs by Peter Hollings

Chatto & Windus · The Hogarth Press
London

Published in 1985 by
Chatto & Windus . The Hogarth Press
40 William IV Street
London WC2N 4DF

Millstone Grit was first published in Great Britain
by Victor Gollancz Ltd 1975
Futura Publications 1977

British Library
CATALOGUING IN PUBLICATION DATA

Hughes, Glyn
    Millstone grit revisited: Glyn Hughes' Yorkshire.
    1. Pennine Chain (England) — Social life and customs
    I. Title
    942.7◇   DA670.P4
    ISBN 0-7011-2960-3

Designed by Alan Bartram
Typeset at The Spartan Press Ltd,
Lymington, Hampshire
Printed by
Butler & Tanner Ltd,
Frome, Somerset

By the same author

PROSE

Millstone Grit
Fair Prospects
Where I Used to Play on the Green
The Hawthorn Goddess

POETRY

Neighbours
Rest The Poor Struggler
Best of Neighbours

PLAYS

Mary Hepton's Heaven

List of illustrations

Acknowledgements

I am grateful for permission to quote from 'The Old Dissent' by Frank Beckwith, collected in F. A. Popham (ed.) *A History of Christianity in Yorkshire* (The Religious Education Press Ltd), and from *Churches and the Working Class in Victorian England* by K. S. Inglis (Routledge & Kegan Paul, 1963). I am particularly grateful to Kenneth Young whose *Chapel* (Eyre Methuen) provided me with the sources of some of the stories of early Methodist conversions.

I must also thank Adelaide Shaw, James Nicholls, William Holt, Charles Chambers, Ernest Hall and the workers at Leigh Mills, Pudsey, for their willing co-operation.

A version of Chapter 3 was first published as 'Calder Valley Mill Families' in the *Illustrated London News*, November 1973.

I

I am writing about, I am living in, that block of the Pennine hills made of millstone grit and ringed by textile towns (or what once were textile towns): Yorkshire wool to the east and Lancashire cotton to the west. Majestic places, they once were. Seen from the hills, the plains now stretch away in a litter of decayed industrial sites and housing estates, like beaches abandoned by the tide.

At night, lights dance in cups and hollows between peninsulas of the moors, from where they are like safe little harbours, filled with the bobbing lights of ships, and joining with the stars to puncture the one velvet fabric of the world and sky.

Millstone grit breaks out of the fields and slopes, as the bones press through the flesh of a hungry cow. In many places – at Blackstone Edge, overlooking Lancashire, at Bride Stones overlooking the Todmorden–Burnley valley, and at Buckstones on the moorland above Marsden where Luddites once drilled, – it rises, swells and towers. Animal and human heads. Huge pregnant stomachs of stone, balanced on slender stems. All manner of reptile, beast, bird and sinewed human forms struggle mightily out of the rushes and the peat, bursting over the crowded industrial valleys below. Places that I haunt, because they embody so much of the spirit of this place. Outcrops that have inspired a great West Yorkshire sculptor, Henry Moore.

The stone is a rough, dark purple, the colour of ripened blackberries. Millstone grit oxidises to this dark tone even without the help of the hundred-year plague of coal soot that has only recently ceased to fall. But break it open, and it is a light and lovely orange or gold sparkling with crystals.

It defines the region of which I write. Northwards, thirty miles away, millstone grit ends at the Aire Gap, beyond which are the limestone Yorkshire Dales. An equal distance south is the limestone of Derbyshire. As one approaches these boundaries, increasing numbers of white stones are to be seen, appearing in the walls of fields and houses. Then the change is sudden. No more cotton or wool-processing towns, which depend upon the rainwater thrown tumultuously *off* millstone grit in a multitude of streams – whereas limestone soaks the water up, becoming riddled with underground caverns. Limestone is gentler, pastoral country.

This millstone grit defines also the nature of the people who dwell on it. Rough, truculent and dour they might appear, but this, as with their stone, is only a forbidding exterior; break it open, and, just as the millstone grit itself is gold inside, so these people sparkle with humour, courage, and kindness.

Abandoned weavers' cottages above the Calder Valley.

A new use for a word has appeared in the Yorkshire vernacular over the past ten years: *real*. No longer does it signify merely 'actual' or 'authentic'. It also means exciting, rich, beautiful, and, above all, *complete*. It has become the superlative for any experience.

'Ow didst tha go on at Shoulder o'Mutton last neet?'

'It were *real*, man. It were real!'

A special Yorkshire development of the word's common use everywhere, as in 'real' ale, 'real' cotton or wool, or, indeed, 'real' life. It suggests something which may be full of disadvantages and lacking in prettiness, but which offers the richness and totality won only from what is authentic; it is the opposite of *kitsch*, in which the unpleasant is left out, thus producing a sentimental and shallow unreality.

And so I call this millstone grit area of England *real*. It is beautiful and dramatic, but doesn't achieve this despite the ugliness, the tragedy and pain of its history – on the contrary, these are part of it.

The people who still dominate this area of the Pennines are the practical nineteenth-century men and women who once made the industrial revolution of steam, coal, machinery, engineering and textiles. They came to crowd a barren moorland region, its villages and slopes then populated only by a scattering of tough-minded independent clothiers. The newcomers were frontiers-people, in need of a new life because they had been displaced by agricultural depression, or by the enclosure of the more fertile common land elsewhere. They were poor and in the late eighteenth century there was money to be made here from the loom; perhaps they were subject to religious persecution as nonconformists, or were hiding from justice amongst the hills. They formed a savage and merciless society. Everywhere, even on the bleakest moortops, the place today is still scarred by the brutalities of the Industrial Revolution. Soot still fouls the grass ten years after the chimneys have gone. Trees will not grow in places once called forests. In Wordsworth's day, the soot of Lancashire stained the air of Lakeland, eighty miles away.

More recently, towns and villages are being marked by what I can only term vandalism – the vandalism of councils or their officers, and that, too, of many cottage-converters, who are allowed to wreck the appearance of villages with incongruous windows, dormer-rooms and garages. Communities are burned and shovelled away, to be replaced by an architectural style that is ubiquitous and abstract; by something done on behalf of all, but which pleases few.

After the pain, tragedy, endurance and heroism of building that society, there is a sense of loss and betrayal throughout the whole of the north of England. It is a forgotten society, without an outlet or a future yet in sight.

There is a feeling here that wealth was made in the nineteenth century, as it was made in more distant colonies; and that the wealth was transported to fight England's foreign wars and to establish the wealth of trading London; and there is a belief that, if life and industry are fading here and money is needed from elsewhere to revive it, then any government money we might receive is no more than a partial repayment of what we have given.

The appearance of Yorkshire, of landscape – or, to use a more profound term, *nature* – is affected by these things concerning the moods, feelings, and histories of the people.

In Greek there is a word, *kaymos*, meaning the longing and misery felt by the exile. The Welsh, similarly, have *hiraeth*.

But their full senses cannot be translated into English, because we do not possess the same history. The English went abroad as exploiters or conquerors, and only nations that know the full pain of exile can plumb these words – except that *kaymos* and *hiraeth* inspire the kind of poetry and song which tears at the inner being, where we all find a matching longing which is spiritual and psychic. It is for whatever lies at the root of the myth of Genesis; it is the pathos of expulsion from the original Garden.

I have some experience of exile. I know what it is to live in a hot dry land, find sprinklers playing on a lawn and be roused, by the sudden smell of damp grass, to an unbearably poignant longing for the little fields stretching down to the stream below my window in Mill Bank near Sowerby Bridge in Yorkshire, with the dew upon them, or after rain. It was for this place, and not for Cheshire, the county of my birth, that I felt the rending of *kaymos*.

My experience of Yorkshire never ceases to be a mixture of sweet and sour. The great beauty of the moorlands and valleys is mixed with the knowledge of their desecration, and one is not to be ignored for the other. The thrill I feel on leaving the motorway from London, and having my first glimpse of stone cottages, with their heavy stone roofs, is mixed with unhappier expectations and understandings. Yet I would not want to be without the latter, which completes the wholeness of the former.

I have lived in West Yorkshire for twenty-five years, but was born on the genteel flatlands of neighbouring Cheshire. A beautiful county, too, but one of eighteenth-century parks and estate farms, woods of beech and oak, lakes, fields of corn and potatoes. Only forty miles to the south-west of here, yet it belongs to a different geographical terrain, and is a whole culture away. No despoliation there, running amok over the landscape. Apparently no savage history, to be dealt with through bitterness or humour; for the land-clearances that preceded the walling of the huge parks, Tatton, Dunham and Tabley, are forgotten, or have become too deeply hidden.

Above all else, Cheshire was private; at any rate, more so than Yorkshire. I was brought up by working-class parents in a council-house estate in Altrincham, which was in fact the last southern tentacle of Manchester and Lancashire. All the industrial and commercial world was at my back (so I thought of it) and as a child I looked in the other direction, over our long garden and the flat fields to the borders of the nearest of Cheshire's great parks: Dunham. My first ventures there were as a trespasser and marauder, one of a gang of housing estate children; and so my first experience of nature was heightened by the thrill of penetrating the private and the secret.

The countryside was guarded by a person whom we named 'Grassy'. He was the mythical Green Man, that spirit of English folklore, who was alive, well and surviving in South Manchester, embodied in the Earl of Stamford's gamekeeper; who once waited for me at a gap in a fence, beating me over my back with his stick as I ran away. He did not quite fit the Grassy of our awestruck talk, who was supposed to have a green skin, green clothes, green hair and a body like a snake when he pounced out of the bushes. My fear of him and my invoking him, especially on the solitary walks that I soon, though I did not know why, began to take, had the effect of intensifying my feeling for nature, which had become a religious experience that was more pagan than Christian.

Then at the age of ten, Romany entered my life. His true name was George Bramwell Evans. He was a renegade Methodist preacher of gypsy blood, who had returned to his caravan and to the bosom of nature. 'Out With Romany' was a radio programme on the BBC's 'Children's Hour' during the 1940s and for a while after the war. Whilst search-lights hunted the night sky, whilst bombs shattered Manchester and Trafford Park, the BBC produced the sound recording of a bird, and 'Why, that's a tree sparrow!' exclaimed Romany. 'Do you mean there's more than one kind of sparrow?' asked the two children who were his disciples. 'Oh yes, there's the common house sparrow and there's the hedge sparrow which has a much sweeter song – why, there's one right now singing his chirpy little melody . . . '

Through Romany, science and knowledge now entered my world, when I joined a local branch of the Romany fan club. Outside Altrincham railway station, in my mother's company one Sunday morning when I was eleven, I met, for the purpose of joining him for a 'nature ramble', Mr Murdoch, a greengrocer; who was also a Romany of my very own. He was dressed in thick rural tweeds. He carried a golfing umbrella (a huge brilliant black and gold thing, like a garden-party tent), a rucksack, and a black tin held with a leather strap. There were two other strange boys, the three of us too shy all day to talk to one another, so I never discovered the fellow passions that had plucked them from their wireless sets. The Romany Society could not have been called a success; yet I, who was to have Mr Murdoch to myself for a long while to come, was beginning one of the significant experiences of my life.

We went to Knutsford, which was ten miles away. As soon as we 'sauntered' (a Romany word, like 'ramble') along the first hedgerow, I expected Nature to reveal Herself as instantaneously as she did through the wireless. Soon, indeed, Mr Murdoch

Fan-club picture of Romany. 'Fields and woods, although the rich man's heritage, may still be the poor man's flower-garden.'

paused, abrupt and intense before various patches of hedge and bankside, and addressed them in Latin. '*Achilea millefolium!*' he said, or '*Digitalis purporea* – the common foxglove.' He would pluck a flower, finger leaves, count petals and stamens. 'A member of the *cruciferae* family,' he might say. From his rucksack he produced a book with pictures of flowers, called, so I learnt, not a 'flower-book', but a 'flora'; and he collected not flowers, but 'specimens', putting them in his tin box, which was called a 'vasculum'. Thus a fresh aspect of Nature entered my life, and She spoke not in a local dialect but in universal Latin.

At one moment Mr Murdoch became excited and, waving his golfing umbrella, left us three standing whilst he raced and stumbled across a ploughed field. Ahead of him a big grey bird lifted into the air, awkwardly buckled its wings, gained height and sailed gracefully away. 'A heron!' he shouted. 'Come on, boys, come on!'

He ran on, but we took no notice. A friendship was at last beginning to stir amongst us, because we all felt embarrassed.

'*Come on!*' Mr Murdoch repeated, alone, unthanked and abandoned in the sticky ploughlands.

The following week, the other boys didn't turn up. It was Mr Murdoch who was embarrassed now, having to face my mother with the inevitable suggestion hanging in the air that something improper had occurred in the fields.

What *were* Mr Murdoch's totally unselfish and unmercenary motives? Why should this greengrocer open up to me his Latin floras, his Victorian manuals of biology, his poetry books (Tennyson, Crabbe), his photography darkroom improvised out of a bathroom, and that attic-laboratory of his which so disgusted his wife with its plates of dried-up earthworms and cockroaches, its stink of formalin?

This man turned out to be one of my finest and most loved teachers. He taught me to read maps and find my way over the footpaths of Cheshire, as well as the arts and sciences of photography and biology; he composed rhyming couplets about our 'rambles', which he published in the local paper, and so he brought me to writing poetry. He taught me to love, observe and identify birds, animals, insects, and thereby he introduced me to the existence of classical culture. He instructed me about geological formations, and the distribution of the stars. I, who was born with few educational advantages, had been granted a private tutor. He was exciting as a teacher because he himself, a man of fifty, was excited to learn (fumbling and ridiculous though he might seem, mispronouncing and misconceiving) through his passionate Sunday hobbies.

What was driving this self-educating Manchester man? Was he an eccentric?

No, he was central to a tradition. Those hordes of rural immigrants, of soldiers demobilised from the Napoleonic Wars – those who, after the French Revolution and the publication of *The Rights of Man*, had been plucked off the common lands or driven to Lancashire and Yorkshire, to learn to weave and for a short while earn high wages – developed a consciousness of their condition, of the cultural inheritance of which they were dispossessed, and found the opportunities to discuss and learn together. The Chartists, the Luddites, the creators of the Co-Operative Movement and of the trade unions; the non- conformist preachers who had the stamina to walk over the moors to preach maybe twenty or thirty times a week to congregations who had sometimes walked twenty miles to hear them; the 'model employers' who built schools and libraries and who worked for factory legislation, and also the working-class mathematicians, scientists, inventors and naturalists, are signs of the extraordinary intellectual activity taking place under appalling conditions.

These are the people who made this northern countryside. John Butterworth of Oldham, born in 1774, who became a spinner at the age of six, who was twenty before he could read and write, who for most of his life was a fustian weaver, but who by 1840 was running his own little school, and who was a contributor to the leading mathematical journals of the day. The anonymous worker of Rochdale, discovered by a factory inspector in 1836, who was so fond of classical learning that he named his children Xanthippe, Diaphantes, and Pandora Barraclough, after the wives of Socrates. Joseph Wright of Idle, Bradford, another who could not read English until he was nearly twenty and who then set about learning as many other languages as he could, before foreign tongues drove him back to his own – not to 'Received Pronunciation', but to the speech of Yorkshire, in love of which he compiled his huge and famous dialect dictionary. The Manchester botanist, James Crowther, born in a cellar in 1768, the son of a labourer, who began work as a drawboy at petticoat weaving, and who after a day's work would sometimes walk twenty miles to collect a specimen of a plant; and John Horsefield, of Besses o'The Barn near Manchester, who learned the Latin names of plants from lists pinned to the post of his handloom.

These were the ancestors of Mr Murdoch. These men gave rise to those weighty Literary Institutes, Lyceums, Mechanics' Institutes, Literary and Philosophical Societies and Temperance Societies that still remain, as significant architecture even if they are now empty of content, in Lancashire and Yorkshire towns. The Royton Temperance Society, founded by a group of young starving workpeople to discover ways of educating themselves during the riots of 1842, and who built their own premises, with a library, maps, a globe, and an organ; the Oldham Botanical Society, whose members paid two pence a month for books, four pence for drink, and by 1795 had twenty volumes and 1,500 plant specimens. (One of its members 'had undertaken a voyage as far as the western parts of America to botanise under the patronage of John Lee Philips of Manchester.')[1]

Their meetings enjoyed huge attendances. At the first public lecture at the Manchester Institute, when the Rev. Andrew Wilson spoke on 'Mechanical Philosophy', 'long before the appointed time every avenue to the theatre was completely blocked up, and when the doors were opened, a tremendous rush took place, and in a

1. C. Aspin, *The First Industrial Society*, Helmshore Local History Society, 1969.

very few minutes the building was crowded to excess'[2] with 1,400 people; the same number had to be turned away.

These men were as inventive in the cause of culture as they were in creating industrial technology. The directors of the Warrington Mechanics' Institute, for instance, bought a one-horse van, filled it with books and sent it once a week to 'every door in Warrington and the vicinity',[3] thus increasing book borrowings from 3,000 to 12,000 books a year.

In *Mary Barton* Mrs Gaskell described 'common hand-loom weavers, who throw the shuttle with unceasing sound, though Newton's "Principia" lies open upon the loom, to be snatched at in work hours, but revelled over in meal times or at night.' She wrote of botanists amongst 'broad-spoken, common-looking factory hands' who are 'equally familiar with either the Linnaean or the Natural system, who know the name and habitat of every plant within a day's walk from their dwellings; who steal the holiday of a day or two when any particular plant should be in flower, and tying up their simple food in their pocket handkerchiefs, set off with single purpose to fetch home the humble-looking weed.' She described the aforementioned James Crowther, who 'notwithstanding all his precautions, was often pursued and had many narrow escapes from being captured. He often contrived to elude his pursuers by his extraordinary swiftness in running. Many were the chases he had, but the most severe was with Mr Hopwood's keepers in Hopwood Park. They once pursued him three or four miles across the country without stopping and he considered it nearly a miracle that he escaped them.'

The working-class Manchester botanist, Richard Buxton – who regularly walked thirty miles in a day to look for plant specimens when he was over sixty years old – introduced his book on the plant life around Manchester by writing, 'fields and woods, although the rich man's heritage, may still be the poor man's flower garden'.[4]

At the same time as I was 'rambling' with Mr Murdoch, at home were stacked the novels of H. G. Wells, and socialist tracts to teach the working man, written by Shaw, Russell, Wells, the Webbs and C. E. M. Joad. These were my father's answer to the confusions that had begun to beset him in his youth, as an out-of-work apprentice engineer. He eventually turned bus conductor. Then, because he was a trade union secretary and organised the bus company's first-ever strike, he was promoted to ticket inspector; this meant that he was paid a salary, which made him ineligible for union membership. (My mother in her insecurity persuaded him to accept this; a classic event of working life.) When he was working a late shift he would spend the morning reading, whilst I was at school and my mother was cleaning other people's houses. At other times he would stay up most of the night in order to educate himself. Often I was awoken by his throwing coal onto the fire, or by his shifting about the kitchen and the room below. I might go downstairs with the excuse of visiting the lavatory

2. *Ibid.*   3. *Ibid.*   4. *Ibid.*

(which was outside in the garden), and find him absorbed in *The New Machiavelli* or *The World of William Clissold*. Then he would keep me from my bed, to talk of Wells, Shaw, and other authors whom he was discovering. I received my first thrill at literature from these two men, my father and Mr Murdoch, themselves caught up in their discoveries.

My father used to send me to the public library to choose books. He too was a natural teacher. He sent me, not because he was too lazy to go there for himself, but because he hoped that I would make my own discoveries amongst the shelves.

I did. I fell upon Richard Jefferies, who first conveyed to me a feeling and admiration for hills, especially in his autobiography, *The Story of My Heart*.

'There was a hill to which I used to resort at such periods. The labour of walking three miles to it, all the while gradually ascending, seemed to clear my blood of the heaviness accumulated at home . . .

' . . . Moving up the sweet short turf, at every step my heart seemed to obtain a wider horizon of feeling; with every inhalation of rich pure air, a deeper desire. The very light of the sun was whiter and more brilliant here. By the time I had reached the summit I had entirely forgotten the petty circumstances and the annoyance of existence. I felt myself, myself.'

What *was* a hill? In Cheshire I had hardly seen one: only midget rises, lifting one a mere few feet over the view. But I already recognised in myself the pantheistic emotions that Jefferies had recorded, and so I desired to see hills, that had caused these feelings in him.

Then my father took me for my first ever glimpse of the Pennines. Using his free bus-pass he took me on excursions, and once he showed me the moors twenty-five miles away at Buxton in Derbyshire. We alighted at a high point, by the Cat and Fiddle Inn – the highest pub in England, I remember him telling me. What emotion I felt when I looked over those grey, round hills slinking through the mist, and saw, for the first time, as if I were a flying bird, stone farms below me, rushes and sparse grass!

And when we walked on, in a breeze so refreshing after the stale air of the bus, to the tiny waterfalls of the Goyt Valley stumbling through red bracken and grey rocks.

It is still with me now as I write, as one of the most powerful emotions of my life, strong as the memory of first making love. We had travelled only twenty-five miles, but no two places could be more different than the countryside south of Manchester and these millstone-grit hills.

But I learnt, when I came to live amongst the Pennines that rise between Lancashire and Yorkshire, that to find here such natural joys unadulterated meant deluding myself.

It meant, too, denying a further richness – that of truth; the truth of the hills as they are; gaunt bleak heads scarred by history.

The Pennines thrill with a powerful, special beauty. Out of some old neglected industrial town, you may climb a hill and be in a world that seems pristine, utterly untouched. In the ever-changing light, the shifting peat bogs that are as formless as putty seem like the soft and shapeless mass of the earth before anything was created upon it.

Perhaps it is a foggy day down below in the towns, and an archipelago of brilliantly lit and coloured hill tops are shifting through the wandering mist. Lie in a hollow in a remote place on the moors. (Emily Brontë thought this one of the greatest pleasures in life.) Through the apparent silence, you distinguish, beyond the song of lark or call of grouse, a continuous hum so constant, monotonous and quiet that you had mistaken it for silence. It is the day-and-night noise of Lancashire and Yorkshire, as incessant as the flow of a river.

One day, on these empty moors where it is possible to walk twenty miles and hardly come across a farmhouse, I tried wiping my fingers along the blades of grass and I found them marked by lines of soot.

In some of the most unlikely, bleak and rocky places, as for instance on the plateau of Saddleworth Moor, black gnarled pieces of tree-root, hardly distinguishable from rock, are embedded in the sour peat. There was once a forest there. That bleak place, thinly covered by a matted hair of grey-yellow grass, its smooth featureless outline marked only by the small eruptions of nineteenth-century coal mining, littered with ice-age boulders and the boulders laid aside after quarrying, with unnatural sheets of water and the Gothic turrets of the Water Board and the old railway company, is still called Denshaw Forest.

On the moors there are mounds, squared-off dykes, low humps of grassed-over stones, looking as ancient as Celtic forts, that are the remains of farmhouses and buildings sunk into the ground within living memory. In one form or another the dereliction of this land has gone on for centuries, and it still continues. Laboriously built walls (now fast breaking down) still divide the hills into small fields, so that you realise they were once important, though now one space of rushes and bog is indistinguishable from another. They were grazing areas, or even fields of tilled earth, the grass and some basic subsistence crops for humans, animals and poultry preciously cultivated against late springs, cool damp summers, and early, vicious winters.

This hilly place between two packed industrial areas, such a joy to the many walkers who love its rough dramas of light and space, is also a man-made desert, exploited, sooted. It is a miniature Sahara or Kalahari; a monument to man's destruction of the natural world.

What a coincidence it is that the images of Hell painted by the pre-industrial artists, Bosch and Breughel, the flaming wastes amongst dark and threatening forms, bear such a striking resemblance to a view from the hills of the industrial valleys of Lancashire and Yorkshire, of Huddersfield, Colne, Rochdale, Burnley and Oldham, that in the nineteenth century made the painters' horrifying visions into palpable realities.

OVERLEAF. 'The Pennines thrill with a powerful, special beauty . . . a world that seems pristine, utterly untouched, like the world before creation.'

2

But let me come down from those heights of the moors and of the mind, where no-one can stay for ever nor probably would wish to remain for long, and introduce you to my village home of Mill Bank.

It is seven miles west of Halifax, in a small valley made by a stream that trickles from the eastern slopes. I fell upon it in 1971, home-hunting with no money to buy even a shed, let alone a house, and no prospect in my feckless way of living of obtaining a mortgage. Yet, helpless and hopeless as I felt, I was not to be disappointed.

I was separated from my first wife and child, with whom I had lived on the other side of the Pennines, and was dwelling for a while in a flat in Manchester. But my joy was that at last, at the age of thirty-six, I was committed to being a poet. Disappointment in marriage had made me reckless enough to give all of myself to it, and everything else now seemed irksome until I had tried myself out. Writing was truly the only thing I wanted to do, so I might as well fail at that as at anything else, I told myself. The commitment acted like the breaking down of a dam on a reservoir. I felt a rush of fluency and authority. Amateurish dithering over my lines gave way to the drive of the professional who feels that it is a matter of life or death to get things right, and I found myself able to publish my first verses.

One spring evening in 1971 I visited a Saddleworth friend. He was working on his cottage, which smelled of fresh sawdust and was littered with tools. My long (it seemed long) immurement in town amongst the car fumes made me sensitive to the spring scents coming from the twilit moorland. I heard a curlew, freshly arrived to nest upon the hills, and what that cry – leisurely, strong, piercing, wistful, questing like a disembodied spirit searching for a thought that it has lost – did to me! If it was calling me invisibly out of the darkness, it certainly worked. When I returned indoors, leaving the moorland scents and cries, into that world conveyed by the smell of sawdust (change, the river of life, turmoil), my mind was made up. I was going back to the hills to carve out a life; to restore a ruined cottage.

There was no shortage of ruins. In between the collapse of Pennine textiles and the rise of the new village-gentility, I was just in time. Post-war governments with grants for the demolition of machinery had hastened the decay of a once-vital industry that had by then grown rigid. As people moved away, leaving behind the aged, the most helpless or the least enterprising, the demolition of towns and villages went along with the dismantling of mills. Yet although the main motorways, including the trans-Pennine (which is only a few miles away) had been built, the potential of such villages as Mill Bank for the commuters of Manchester and Leeds had not been

Mill Bank, dominated by the chapel. Home is between the telephone-post and the hornbeam tree on the right. '. . . the brief sense of an Eden; the village and cottage of my heart.'

developed. In the meanwhile, for a short time at least, I have enjoyed the brief sense of an Eden; of the village and cottage of my heart.

I lived temporarily in Hebden Bridge. I combed paths and neglected tracks for derelict houses, because with my resources it was no use my going to an estate agent. How I would purchase or provide for what I found, I did not know, any more than I understood why faith should drive me in such a hopeless search.

Instinct sent me along the ancient packhorse-ways that link the main villages (called here always 'towns'), hanging at the point where the springs pour and gather sufficient water for a community, half-way between the exposed hill tops and what were marshes or summer meadows in the valley bottoms. So I walked through Heptonstall, Midgeley, Luddenden and Sowerby. Old towns, small and stony, huddled to protect themselves from violent weather, amongst what had once been wasteland and had then become the small walled enclosures of domestic weavers and spinners, high above the industrial communities in the valleys that they are parent to: Hebden Bridge, Luddenden Foot and Sowerby Bridge. The hillsides are spread with a web of stony tracks, some linking farms, hamlets and chapels, whilst others stretch erratically straight like long ash-grey broken limbs across miles of moorland; all necessary for the clothiers who had to take their wool, either on their own backs or on packhorses, between the many places where it was processed – spinner, weaver, fulling mill – and the 'piece hall' where it was sold.

I inquired into cottages in Heptonstall, but rejected them because at £250 they were too expensive for me even to think about, and were damp. I chased after collapsing farms on a grouse moor, apparently left to decay in order not to interfere with the shooting. I wasted my energies on farmers who could never finally work out how best to take advantage of me. I negotiated lengthily with lonely old people who merely wanted someone to talk to and to pass away the time.

From Crow Hill, above Sowerby, I descended at last upon Mill Bank.

It lies in a vulva of trees sunk into the flank of the moors. The village is on one slope only, facing the woods. The houses are packed in between an eighteenth-century woollen mill (now converted into flats) at the bottom of the hill by the stream, and the Methodist Chapel and Sunday School (also now changed into houses), that crown Mill Bank like the wedges of two huge gravestones. The chapel where Paraffin Willey (a Sunday-School teacher who 'hawked' paraffin for a living) frightened the children with his shadowy home-made lantern slides of the denizens of Hell; and the mill in the entrance of which a large Bible was turned to a fresh page daily, for the spinners and weavers to pause over as they passed into work. Mill and work at bottom, chapel and Heaven at top, and the wild moors surrounding all.

The stones of Mill Bank were golden when they were quarried. They spent a century dark with soot, and now in the post-mill age have patchily bleached to a mixture of black and gold, in autumn rains sometimes green with moss. Almost all the houses are without gardens. They open direct into lanes, alleyways and steep flights of open stone stairs. You as often look over roofs as at walls, and these stone tiles and chimneys are part of the beauty. Especially is this so when they glitter, running with silver, after a rain shower.

Mill Bank is an old village (its corn mill mentioned in the Domesday Book) created where a branch of a Roman trans-Pennine route, the Blackstone-Edge road, crossed the stream. But in the mid-nineteenth century almost all of it was rebuilt as workers' dwellings during the textile boom. Blocks with the immense heartless grandeur of the mills themselves were erected. The result was a typical Yorkshire architectural compromise with rocky outcrops, gorges and hillsides. There are many houses in this district which are entered on street level at one side, whilst at the back of the 'ground floor' room you find yourself above a two- or even three-storied cottage, staring over packed roofs at woods and spacious moors under their dancing lights or at the rushing effects of wind and rain.

The village was Methodist-inspired. The chapel dominates it, but there is no Anglican or any other variety of chapel or church nearer than a mile's distance. Socially and spiritually Mill Bank was dependent upon the chapel, whilst economically for a hundred years it relied upon the several mills spaced along the length of the stream and the river. Throughout West Yorkshire, mill, chapel and house represented a common and unified culture; the chapel gravestones and the mill gates have the same monumental styles. Yes, that culture sank its roots into the European Renaissance, and beyond that into Greece and Rome; but for better or for worse it was transformed, through the isolation of these valleys (though their woollen-worsted conquered the world) into something individual, local and appropriate.

One mill here is still in business. Half a mile across the fields it is visible through my window, harboured deep in woods and hills, and when lit at night it is like a great liner cruising through the heavy waves of moorland. Old people remember when no-one owned a clock, but everyone looked across at the mill tower, which in any case, before the age of radio time-checks, held authority, like God, over time. They remember too that on winter dawns, and on dark evenings, the old ones and the nursing mothers left at home could see long processions of lights swaying through the wood to and from the mill.

But when I discovered Mill Bank the village was in decay, the houses empty. It had a reputation as the haunt of bad rentpayers and of the clients of the magistrates' bench. The little mill at the foot of the village had just gone bankrupt. Many cottages had already been demolished. Ugly stone and weed-strewn gaps that had become rubbish dumps were overlooked by the shattered remains of what had once been interior walls. Private things, wallpapers and bedroom fireplaces, were displayed in unseemly fashion. Half a dozen public houses had been shut down. The working men's club, the chapel, and the Sunday school were closed. The chip shop, the cobbler's and the barber's were no more than legendary examples of the public facilities that had once existed. Only the school (DEO ECCLESIA PAUPERIBUS AD 1850) and the little post office survived.

And here, amongst the derelict cottages of this beautiful and at that time peaceful village, one which just because of the neglect of the past ten years was *unspoilt*, I found (a poet alone with no money in his pocket) my home.

It was boarded up. Neighbours, brought onto the street through curiosity, told me who owned it. A local haulage firm had bought it for one of their drivers who needed a house in a hurry, and after a few years he and his wife moved to something that they thought was better. The cottage had a closing order upon it – which meant that no one could live in it again unless certain improvements were made.

I had nothing to lose. I went to see the manager, who was amazed that anyone should want it, and thought I'd see more sense when I'd been inside.

'Yer can look it over if you like,' he said, 'but yer'll not want it. Council's planning demolishing of it.'

'I'd like to see it,' I insisted.

'It's boarded up, isn't it?'

'I'll nail it up again.'

'Look it over if you like. But yer'll not want it,' he repeated.

I borrowed a hammer and pincers to pull out the six-inch nails that held the front door. This once more brought out a neighbour. 'Nobody's lived there for about seven years,' she said, with melancholy. 'They took the 'lectric wiring as well. You can't leave anything these days.'

Damp bills and debt-collectors' mildewed letters lay behind the door. I wrenched a plank from the downstairs window to let the light onto the stone floor. Beyond the first room was another tiny one, without windows, smelling of urine and holding a kitchen sink. 'That'll be the coal 'ole,' said the woman, who with her children had followed me in.

The coal was shot straight from the street on the far side of the house into the windowless kitchen, with nothing but a bit of wood to hold it back. A stone staircase led upstairs to a single bedroom. One floorboard was shredded into soft woolly splinters where water had got in through the ceiling. There was a small, simple and yet exquisite stone fireplace.

But most of all I loved the woods, fields and hills I could see through the window. I have looked at that view for fifteen years now and have not tired of it. Studying it closely, I never found it the same for two minutes together. It changes constantly under the effects of season, light, wind, sun and rain.

I ignored the cellar, nailed the door up again, and went back to the mill manager, prepared to bargain, and terrified of losing my house.

'There's no electricity nor water in there,' I said.

'That's reet.'

'The floorboards are rotten. It needs new window frames.'

'That's reet. I knowed from t'start tha'd not want it.'

'I'll offer you fifty pounds.'

A long slow stare.

'Whatever dusta want it for?'

I can't think how I might describe what I found, without making it seem like a slum. And yet what was in that cottage is typical of the way that the working people of Yorkshire were expected to live and bring up their children whilst they were producing the finest and most sought-after woollens in the world.

It was an 'under-and-over' and 'back-to-back' house. That is, it involved an intricate and confusing interlocking of one cottage with another. Despite my later improvements, visitors still find its geography confusing. Although my own toilet was outside, thirty yards away up the street, a neighbour's small bathroom had been contrived above my bedroom ceiling. There was no mention of this on any deeds – it was simply a trespass. The waste pipes crossed my ceiling to fall down an iron pipe. (It had a lacy iron cover, which I later saved from a builder's skip to place on my mantelpiece and set with dried flowers.) When lying in bed I had to listen to the sliding, *glug glug*, across the ceiling.

Yet how much (given the advantages of being poor in the late twentieth century) have I loved this cottage, bought with borrowed money, and its surroundings!

How peaceful Mill Bank was, and, in its untransformed but also unadulterated state, satisfying to look over! Throughout its day it enjoyed spasms of life like the sporadic jerking of a dying animal. For an hour before eight a.m. a few old vans departed, creaking and groaning. Boots slurred by. Then quiet: and I love quiet the more because I live in an age that appreciates it so little; one of audio-pollution that is ignored more than other environmental adulterations. I was able to listen to the pleasant sounds of birds, wind, rain, or sporadic human noises: the postman, the milkman or forlorn door-to-door sales people combing their most desperate beat. Council-workers parked in the secret lanes for lengthier than usual lunch hours. And for brief moments, indeed, the first signs of Mill Bank's future emerged. Men seeking 'business lunches' dashed through Mill Bank, in cars sprayed the faint colours of ice-creams, to public houses that were once remote, their bars as greasy as old gas stoves, but which are now like airport lounges.

Uncertainty over the future caused even greater squalor. The village was likely to be demolished and replaced with one of those council house estates that look so barren, ugly and conspicuous on a Pennine hillside. No-one wanted to give time or money for the 'doing up' of these inadequate houses, so they remained empty and had their windows broken, their fixtures and electric wiring wrecked, their water and gas supplies plundered for the sake of copper and lead piping. With good fortune, some cottages were boarded up. The result was depressingly desolate.

There were plagues of untidiness. One family would begin by stacking old car tyres, an old gas stove or an unwanted chair outside its door – if the Cleansing Department wouldn't move them, if you had neither a car of your own nor money to hire someone else to take them to the Corporation tip, and if you had no land on which to burn or bury them, what else could you do? A dustbin would overflow, or a dog would learn to lift the lid with its nose and upset the rubbish into the street. Often it began with a lapse because of the difficulty of tidying up after children who had only the street in which to play. No sooner had the filth begun to gather in the gutters and flow around the village, than others would catch on to the pointlessness of keeping dustbins tidy. Soon, the vicinity of the 'ash-yard', the lavatories, and eventually the whole village, would smell of neglected drains and stale food.

The poet kept on writing at no 28. I dreamed of restoring it to the basic nature of a weaver's cottage, of keeping it in unity with what had already been created; stone floors, dark cupboards and open fires were precious to me. In the chapel and the Sunday school my friend, an artist, worked. The members of the John Bull theatre group were scattered around. All of us had drifted to this corner of Yorkshire for the same reasons: partly attracted by its cheapness, and partly by the Mill Bank magnetism, as if this beautiful secret place was intended for us. Most of us were fleeing from unhappy marriages. None of us was much 'known' or successful. My friends of that time, who made Mill Bank such a warm and supporting community, have since become disillusioned in their hopes for the village and have left, whilst I have stayed on to hear it called, by an estate-agent's clerk, 'the poet's village'. It was like reading my own obituary. But before this happened, and whilst Mill Bank tottered, tumbled or gasped with hope, these people were the ones with whom to spend evenings, to go fishing for trout, to turn to for help or for laughter, to borrow tools from, to drink with, and then perhaps, as we did so often late at night, go for a curry in Bradford, nine miles away, where some of the best food I know of is to be had in either of two Indian cafés, one on each side of the Public Mortuary.

It was the persistence of a few in the village who organised meetings, wrote letters to the newspapers, searched out allies and put forward persuasive arguments, that saved Mill Bank from the gulf of total disappearance. Mill Bank became a 'General Improvement Area' and, although for years few had wanted to live here, now the builders were seeking permission to erect houses and complaining of the 'selfishness' of anyone who objected to their plans. Many of those who had originally lived here chose to go onto a housing estate. I stayed tight, and have watched the village fill with well-heeled strangers: smart cars, cottages 'improved' with plastic soil-pipes and box-shaped loft-conversions wrecking the roof-lines, even peacocks fluttering about the streets and roofs.

As I write this, there is a scheme under way to purchase the former chapel by my back door and convert it into a 'Witches' Temple'. The council officers have already pointed out that planning permission and a car park would be necessary; as I'm right on the flight path, I'm now thinking of turning my cellar into a broomstick park, and doing bats' bed-and-breakfast in the attic. It's all part of the continual turmoil and change, I tell myself, that has always been typical of West Yorkshire.

I, too, put my eager hands upon some grant aid, and 'converted' my cottage. Whilst it took place, I lit a fine bonfire of the detritus of my life so far, and went to the house of my friends David and Tina Pease in Todmorden. I planned to do something I had never done, but have felt for years that I ought to do: to find out what these borders of Yorkshire and Lancashire, that I knew so well from driving around them, and from one-day walks, would look like and feel like if I hiked them for many days on end.

People walk for different reasons, the most common being for the sake of exercise. Northerners, at any rate, often go out in a spirit of claiming their rights to land, air, and freedom; a spirit that lies behind the traditional socialist-hikers of Lancashire and Yorkshire, and which culminated in the famous 'Battle of Kinder Scout', when they fought with gamekeepers on the hills outside Glossop, and which led to the first access-to-the-countryside act.

Another reason for walking is, simply, for contemplation, and that is generally my purpose. I am a starer. Dawdling, looking carefully, won't give you much physical exercise, but there is a deep spiritual fulfilment in it.

3

Todmorden is ten miles away along the River Calder. One afternoon at the end of winter I drove a van overloaded with boxes of my most valued possessions, my papers and books, along the road at the bottom of the deep glacial valley which forms the axis of this region. It splits the Pennines, but links Lancashire with Yorkshire, and is always the last route to be closed by the snow. The river has been called 'the hardest worked in England', because of the number of mills along its banks. Road, railway and canal have in their day been pretty busy, too. They are all plaited in the cramped sump of a valley where the dark towns of Lancashire and Yorkshire intermingle, like threads of spun cotton or wool.

At the end of the valley, the division between the counties is subtle. Todmorden, on the border, expresses the uncertainty of identity. It has brick cotton mills, a sight typical to Lancashire, and there is also something very Lancashire in the more sprightly, less dour cast of Todmorden humour; but its oldest and strongest tendencies are towards Yorkshire. This unsureness, and the town's natural allegiance, are expressed well in a Todmorden joke. A lady, uncertain which county she lived in, inquired at the post office, and when told that she was in Yorkshire, replied, 'Thank God for that! I believe they have terrible weather in Lancashire.'

The valley is an unhealed wound, narrow and deep like a razor cut. It is so deep, sharp and narrow, that in some places you may cross the nearby moors and be unaware that it exists. There you are on a plateau of wild, sooted grass, here and there sinking into a misty hollow or erupting in a cluster of stones; a wilderness so free and open that, being human, you search the horizon for something else that is human – a tiny speck of a farmhouse, or a church, or a distant hamlet. You see a pub in the distance and think you will cross the bog in fifteen minutes. But a column of smoke lifts out of a crack in the earth; and rising out of the ground, like a spike, is the tip of a church steeple. Suddenly you are pitched into the valley. A great hole is clanking, hissing and spitting fire beneath your feet – a vision by Dante, Blake or Hieronymus Bosch.

'The Athens of the Industrial Revolution', such places have been called. Buildings marked with the confidence and certainty that they were making something great and new. They represent the apotheosis of sheer labour, and the weight of that God is overawing. I think of the 367–foot chimney that was built in sixteen weeks at Blinkhorn's chemical works, Bolton, in 1842 ('a circumstance unparalleled in the history of the world,' crowed *The Bolton Chronicle*), up which 4,000 people were hauled, four at a time in a basket, to admire the view from the top before the chimney was used; or the 435–foot chimney built in 1846 at Wallgate, Wigan, but which

'I climbed onto the rim of a plateau . . . the noises of the Calder Valley were suddenly shut off. A different world . . . a maze of tiny, stone-walled fields.'

collapsed into the canal, so that a man on the bank who fell in was driven to the other side by waves created by the falling stone.

Now much of the industry in the Calder Valley has retreated and left a mess of streets, useless mills, and portentous public buildings, like litter in the path of a flood. Out of this industry a few families became incredibly wealthy; by now some of them have sunk back into the poverty from which, so meteor-like, they sprang. 'From clogs to clogs again in three generations,' as the local saying has it. Nonetheless, those half dozen or so families had a dramatic influence on the landscape, on the character of the town and the culture of the people. They represent, in their different ways, Yorkshire at its grandest, or should I say, most grandiloquent.

You might expect the Fieldens, the Cockcrofts, the Rawsons, the Stansfields and the Wheelwrights who governed these valleys to have had a similar life-style and influence. In fact their differences are shown by variations in the very landscape on which they bore their patriarchal, God-like influence; for the inner spirit of people does influence the land.

At Todmorden, the hillsides reaching from the streets by the greasy river and canal, up to the lip of the valley, are shattered and scarred, like a still smouldering battlefield. But ten miles away down the valley near Mill Bank, the mills are subtly contained in an eighteenth-century landscape (admittedly grown ragged now) of parkland with gracious, if neglected houses, set next to or above the mills.

The grandest of the houses near Mill Bank is Field Place, built by George Stansfield in 1749. It is the kind of mansion that was erected by a young aristocrat who had been on the Grand Tour, thus acquiring a tasteful knowledge of Palladian styles: it boasts (that is exactly the right verb) a pedimented front with two symmetrical wings. The Stansfields grew rich from the 'domestic system for woollens'. At the back of Field House is a courtyard surrounded by warehouses in which were stored the pieces of cloth woven at hill farms and collected by the master clothier. There are dye-shops and cropping-sheds. In the eighteenth century, the now insignificant lane that runs across the front was as important as a modern motorway; a branch of the Roman road that was known as the Blackstone Edge Road, it then became the packhorse route that crossed the Pennines and took the Stansfields' cloth to their distant customers. The Stansfields, marrying into the Rawsons and other families of the local squirearchy, developed into bankers, patrons of the arts (they supported Branwell Brontë in his excesses), and millowners. In accordance with the eighteenth-century tradition, the factories that they built later were seen as appendages to the domestic offices. For instance, at the cobbled approach to Brockwell (one of the family homes) are two gates side by side; one leads onto terraced lawns before the house, which has two huge bay windows facing towards the sun and the pastoral valley, whilst the other turns into dark passageways between slimy, shadowy mill buildings at the back of the house, and then to a group of farm sheds. It seems indecent – how could they insult their victims so? The great bay windows were added in the early nineteenth century and I

A seventeenth century master-clothier's home near Heptonstall. '. . . a long and heavy house with fine masonry in window mullions, corbels and porches.'

imagine that as mill life became more awful, so the house developed these two great, popping eyes straining away towards the sun and over the hills.

The Rawsons built several such units of farm, mill and house in the valley. They believed that 'trade follows the flag', and the sons who did not remain in the textile industry, quite literally 'planted the flag' overseas; Admiral Sir Harry Holdsworth Rawson was military commandant of Cyprus when it was ceded to the British and he hoisted the first official British pendant there. Christopher Rawson ran away to sea and, having 'gloriously served' the East India Company, returned to found the Halifax Literary and Philosophical Society, exhibiting there a collection of Roman coins and 'Greek marble figures'.

The story of the Rawsons, the Stansfields and the Wheelwrights at this end of the valley is of distinguished military careers abroad; at home, of petty snobbery, combined with self-help and with pastoral care for the valley and its people. Dorothy Rawson, who is still alive, learnt to make jam and bread, and to sew her own dresses; whilst on the home farm she was taught the arts of the slaughter-house. When her father was courting her mother, if they were out too late their parents had the church bells rung. (*These* were Anglicans!) A Rawson planted one thousand trees in the valley. They took soup to sick villagers. At Christmas and at Whitsuntide the villagers came in procession and were given traditional gifts: a bag of sweets at Mill House, an orange at Haugh End. The Stansfields rebuilt Sowerby Church and took the medieval one to decorate their garden. When Mrs Wheelwright drove out she expected girls to curtsey to her, and when Mrs McDougal-Rawson drove recklessly to church in her dog cart she assumed the right to flick people out of her way with her whip.

These families, whose origins were in the mid-eighteenth century, were tasteful in art (in the aristocratic sense), and took care of architecture and landscape through their traditional notions of beauty. They were paternalistic. Yet they were insensitive to the economic conditions which they themselves imposed upon the working population of the district.

On the other hand, those who became wealthy at the other end of the valley began their careers, and rose out of the common stock, only slightly later, at the very end of the century – and yet they belonged to a different age, when the Industrial Revolution was already under way. Their style was practical and philistine. But the best of them preserved their understanding of and sympathy for the class on which they depended and out of which they had sprung.

The original Cockcroft, for example – a man called 'Jack O'Th'Heights' – was a 'moor-edger', that is, one who scratched a living at a small farm on the edge of the moor. He made a fortune quickly by renting a shed in the valley that was ready-provided with power for looms. And all his descendants have proved equally pragmatic; Sir John Cockcroft, for instance, gained his Nobel Prize for Physics because he found the *practical* way to split the atom.

This sudden birth of a new age, when such as the Cockcrofts profited from river-side,

Kershaw House, Luddenden Foot, Calderdale, built 1650.

power-driven sheds, was occasioned by the failure of Richard Arkwright, the inventor of a spinning machine, to maintain his patents at the end of the eighteenth century. Investors in the north had been anticipating this and were poised with bankers' and company capital to begin the mill-building that swamped the Lancashire and Yorkshire valleys during the following decade.

The largest profits of all were made by the Fielden brothers of Todmorden. The original Fielden was also one who left a farm on the edge of the rocks to establish a cotton business in a block of three cottages. His sons began life with hard labour spinning cotton in this primitive factory at an early age, yet they were eventually reckoned to be amongst the richest men in the world – exceeding even the riches of their fellow cotton-spinners by investing in West Indian sugar.

Their notion of tasteful art was the town hall that they paid for in their native town. Its pediment, based on that of the Parthenon, displays pseudo-Greek figures carrying an engine crank-shaft, a box of spindles, and a bale of cotton. Another example of their taste was the immodestly-named Dobroyd Castle: an immense, forbidding display of black stone built in 1866 by John Fielden.

(John was, it is said, in competition with his brother Joshua for the hand of one of their mill girls, Ruth, who promised to marry the first one to build a castle for her. After her wedding to John he sent her to be refined at a finishing school in Switzerland. On her return, she was unhappy in this castle which she had commanded her husband to build. She retired to a 'Swiss chalet' in the grounds, and there she died of drink.)

'Vulgar' as John Fielden might have been, when he became a Member of Parliament he laboured with his friend Cobbett for a Bill reducing the hours worked in factories. Westminster was not an easy place for him. As the *Dictionary of National Biography* puts it, ' . . . he did not shine as an orator. His voice was very weak; he spoke with a strong provincial accent, and neither his elaborate industrial statistics nor the minute details of his descriptions of distress in the manufacturing districts were appreciated by the house.' Fielden, though a factory-owner, proposed an eight-hour day, which was an impossible ideal for that Parliament; but he did achieve victory with the Ten Hour Act, which earned him the title of 'Ulysses of The Ten Hour Act', and a statue in Todmorden erected by subscription from the factory operatives themselves. Engels considered him to be an 'honourable exception' to his class; and when the 'plug drawers' moved up the valley from Rochdale, removing the plugs from the factory boilers and thus releasing their heads of steam, they left Fielden's mill untouched.

The time which separates the building of Field Place and of Dobroyd Castle covers the period of William Blake's life, which was from 1757 to 1827. It has often seemed to me that he was, as it were, born at one end of the Calder Valley and prophesied the others:

'I have blotted out from light and living the dove and the nightingale,
And I have caused the earthworm to beg from door to door . . .

My heavens are brass, my earth is iron, my moon a clod of clay,
My sun a pestilence burning at noon, and a vapour of death in the night.'

4

My friends the Peases live on one of the hillsides above Todmorden, in Kilnhurst, a long and heavy house with fine masonry in window mullions, corbels and porches, once a master-clothier's home. I unpacked my van and prepared myself for an afternoon spent, perhaps, in catching the last of the sun in the garden and an evening of log-fire, wine, good food, and late night talk.

Kilnhurst belonged to William Holt (another bon vivant of a rare but local breed) until his divorce at the age of eighty; then he went to live in the neighbouring barn with his horse Trigger that had carried him on 20,000 miles of journeys through France, Italy, Austria, Germany and the Netherlands.

Above the house, where a hollow trapped the March sun, the horse stood with its friend Billy lying between its feet. True to his exotic pose, he was wearing a panama hat and riding breeches. A man with the stunted stature of generations of mill-workers, he had escaped the factory, and was reading Milton's *Paradise Lost* in the grass above a mill-town that was as active as Hell's furnace, clanking and spitting fire beneath him.

An independent spirit and auto-didact, he was; the author of ten books (autobiography, *I Haven't Unpacked*, *I Still Haven't Unpacked*, *Trigger in Europe* etc; and novels, *The Weaver's Knot*, *The Wizard of Whirlaw* and others) as well as journalism – especially from the battle fronts of the Spanish Civil War, the Russian Revolution, and the north of England – and of innumerable radio broadcasts, during and after the Second World War.

He was born of the work ethic at its severest, when in Todmorden at the age of twelve he went half-time from school to train as a weaver. But it was also what inspired and powered the work ethic (that is, non-conformism) that gave Billy the impulse and the means to self-education, reflection, and freedom. Distinctively a rebel, yet Billy is still so steeped in non-conformism that it is natural to him, for example, to introduce a character in one of his books as 'a local Rechabite official, Band of Hope leader, and temperance reformer' – terms now meaningless to almost anyone under middle age.

The main intellectual force in Todmorden was Unitarianism: a high brow form of non-conformism that added ingredients of Reason and of modern scientific knowledge. (It was, incidentally, the faith of John Fielden.) In Billy Holt's make-up, non-conformist values and their antithesis were present at his birth and rivalled one another until the end of his life. His father was an itinerant folk-fiddler, tamed to Wesleyanism and to playing his fiddle only in the church choir by the woman he married. (A story, or a tragedy, that could be repeated through a thousand examples in the history of the north). And yet like Billy himself he could not lose his wildness completely, but remained restless, living by 'hawking' coal from door to door; in and out of debt, and constantly changing addresses. Father and mother took the Temperance Pledge, and so did Billy (breaking it, with famous excess, from his time in the Somme battlefield onwards). Mother sang in the chapel choir. The great mentor of Billy's youth was a local Unitarian bookseller. There were Bible Discussion groups, the Unitarian Sunday School Amateur Operatic Society, etc.

Yet it was this same non-conformism which became the springboard for Billy's wildest flights of ideas, and for his rebellious mysticism; what his divorced wife Florence called his 'magic Methodism', exemplified in his large painting, 'Christ Overcoming Time and Space', which hung in the stable shared by Trigger and himself; his passion for the Fourth Dimension; his search for 'the meaning that lay behind things'; and his insistence on beginning his will with the words '*If* I die' (since no-one could prove the inevitability of his death), despite the quarrels it brought him with solicitors. Billy described himself as 'a non-conformist who couldn't conform with the non-conformists.'

The same tension, between a feckless wandering husband and a mother tied to the home, was reflected in his own marriage. Florence was from Barnsley, a South Yorkshire coal town where the choice for a girl (according to Flo) was between 'domestic service, and the sweat-shops of the corduroy manufacturers.' Her father was a collier, and the booming cotton industry in Todmorden attracted him with its opportunities for his daughter. There he worked as a road-mender, whilst she became a winder in a spinning mill. She was famous for her beauty, and Billy captured her when he returned from the trenches of the First World War. He had been one of the few working men selected for officer training, but he fell out of a window whilst celebrating the end of hostilities and broke his legs; it was the only injury he sustained throughout the war, though it put an end to his ambitions as an officer, and returned him to Todmorden.

Or did she capture him? She told him that she was pregnant. They were hurriedly married. The famous traveller and his bride went by bus for a honeymoon at nearby Hardcastle Crags, and Florence gave birth to a daughter only five months after Billy had returned to England. The child was called Florence Dolores, after her mother, and pain.

Billy did more travelling after his marriage than he had practised before it: the last of his travels being the long journey with the horse which he discovered in the 1950s pulling a rag and bone cart through Todmorden, and bought for five pounds. Billy's version of their meeting is that the horse seemed as unhappily blinkered between the shafts as he was at that moment by the dark hills closing in the Calder Valley, and it seemed only right that they should go on an adventure together.

'When fate stares you in the face, don't run away from it. Seize it with both hands and polish it,' he said.

Later, with my tape-recorder set up on his kitchen table, I recorded Billy's account of his life. There he addressed the little machine produced from the pocket of my rucksack as grandly as if he was once again speaking into a BBC microphone during the Battle of Britain.

'I was an offspring of the pioneers of the Industrial Revolution, the weavers and the spinners who took the blitz of the machines, that came out of space to them, on the chin, and now they lie under the sod. They haunt me, the spirits of those men and women and even children who had to take this terrible invasion of the machinery into their lives. Those weavers and spinners haunt me, the mill-wrights and engineers and early pioneers of the Industrial Revolution who carried on almost ignored by the rest of the world who were too concerned with Dionysus and the Napoleonic Wars and all kinds of things that were happening south of this region.

'Right before the pyramids of Egypt, all through human history, two hands had spun one thread with the spinning wheel. This extends to the time of George Washington. Then there came a man, almost illiterate, a weaver, who spun eight threads and then spun ten threads and then eighty threads and then 120 threads, with only two hands – one hand turning the wheel and the other hand drawing out the cotton. That was James Hargraves, and until recently there wasn't even a plaque, let alone a monument recording his name, but a few years ago a fuss was made by a few people like me and a small garden of remembrance has been made near where he was born just above Oswaldtwistle. As the crow flies it's only about ten miles from where we're sitting now in this barn, so we're practically within the cradle of the Industrial Revolution. Because these extra threads were spun by turning a handle on this machine made of bits of wood and brass it was possible to speed up production and this led to water frames and frames driven by steam engines. And even now in this region there's this curious engineering character of the old mill-wrights who applied science to practical life. Sir John Cockcroft, who helped split the atom and really found the philosopher's stone, turning baser metals into gold, was born in Todmorden – Sir John Cockcroft, and a fellow called Wilkinson, a chemist. Isn't that amazing? – and there isn't a memorial to either of them. Cockcroft, when he lived round here as a boy, built an electric system into their mill, John Cockcroft and Sons at Walsden. I knew him very well and he was sorry its spin-off was the atom bomb.

'Right from my earliest days my thoughts were rebellious against authority. The first authority was my family. Before I could even talk I ran away several times. Once my mother tied me to the railings outside our little terraced house in Joshua Street and one of my aunts who was sorry for me released me.

'The authority of the school came next, because it was boring. My parents sent me to school very early to get what they called discipline. Discipline was to stop you being what you really are, that is it was the opposite of education – instead of drawing

Billy Holt and Trigger. 'I'm not dissatisfied. But I'm unsatisfied. Unsatisfied means
you like what's on the menu but there isn't enough of it.'

out of you what you are, they tried to make you into something else. They sent me when I was three, and I wouldn't have it. There was an attempt to discipline me by using the cane. This inspired my first work of art, a mural decoration. When they put me to bed I got out my materials and drew the teacher with a cane in her hand and extended the cane all the way round the four walls of the bedroom to the back of the teacher where there was a small boy receiving the punishment. That was my first work of art, inspired by rebellion. I was about three.

'I revolted against theology in the Sunday Schools. I was deeply religious in that I was fascinated by the mystery of existence: Who was I? Why was I here? What was it all about? I wasn't satisfied by the explanation given by my Sunday School teacher, who was a non-conformist Wesleyan. I objected to all the stuff that was wrapped around Jesus. It was quite simple to understand what he said, it all seemed quite reasonable to me, but there was such a lot of talk about the others in the Bible, especially St Paul. He was quite a person was St Paul, writing letters to explain all sorts of things. I said, "Yes, I know. I take it for granted. Why bother about all that? Let's get back to Jesus." Because I kept getting back to Jesus' "Sermon On The Mount" and so on, my Uncle Will, who was a Sunday School teacher, said I was drifting towards Unitarianism – Unitarianism looks upon Jesus as a human person and doesn't bother much about his supernatural origins. But I'm not a Unitarian. I'm what you might call a non-conformist who doesn't conform with the non-conformists – that's a funny sort of rebellion, isn't it?

'What I do remember is the old second-hand bookseller who was the principal teacher of the young men's class. He was a very sincere fellow and he gave this extraordinary apology for St Paul. He said, "Thou'rt after a bare-legged religion, art tha'? Thou wouldn't go down the street without thee breeches on, wouldst tha'?" "No," I answered. "Then let thee dress thy religion up," he said. "The glory of Jesus will shine through all the wrappings that either thee or St Paul can put around him."'

'And right enough, the glory of Jesus does shine through every attempt to decorate him or veil him or transfigure him. Even John Wesley, for instance. Though he was a Conservative and a reactionary he couldn't hide the teaching of Jesus.

'When I was twelve I began half-time at the mill. One week I had to work mornings starting at six o'clock, and then on alternate weeks I worked afternoons. Like the other half-timers I felt sleepy when I went to school in the afternoon. The teachers put all the half-timers on the back row and if we fell asleep they didn't wake us. So I didn't learn much at school. I went full-time to the mill when I was thirteen and then I had to work fifty-six hours a week – ten hours a day, and Saturday mornings.

'The noise of the machinery of weaving is a monotonous roar, so loud that you can't hear your own voice even if you shout; people communicate by lip-reading like deaf-and-dumb people. This noise became like a silence to me; nobody could interrupt me. I could think for hours and hours at a time. I was out in the wilderness, alone like the Old Testament prophets. I began to learn languages, for their sheer beauty. I didn't care about examinations and I'd no plans but I wanted to read the classics in the original and the great writers in all the different languages. I started with German, because the Gothic letters were so beautiful. I was able to recite German in the roar of the looms without anyone skitting me; they couldn't hear what I was saying and they couldn't lip-read either, because it was German.

'There's a constant falling of dust from cotton weaving. It's part of the size and the china clay. Like you can write on a mirror when you breathe on it, you can write in the dust that falls on the steel machines, then rub it off and soon the dust settles again. I wrote my first exercises in German in that dust.

'After the discipline of school, and the mill, there was the discipline of the army, in 1914. I didn't much mind that, there was action and we were fighting for some purpose. The army released me from this valley and gave me an opportunity to use my talents. One thing it insisted upon was: never let the enemy take the initiative, you take it and you'll always be right.

'In writing home to my mother and father I began to be interested in what was coming into my own letters when I described a cabbage field in the rain looking like scales. I thought it was nice to think of things like that so I developed letter-writing in the army.

'I dived into politics in that period when the winds of change were blowing pretty violently. I met a lot of prominent politicians, Harry Pollitt and so on. Many of them visited my home and all I could give them was bread and butter, and not even that sometimes. My joining the Communist Party was speeded up by the debate that took place in Parliament on Socialism. They said that Socialism wouldn't work because human nature wasn't good enough. There's a certain amount of truth in it – I know that human nature is bewildered, ignorant, and has been very unkindly treated. But I have great faith in human nature in its deepest state: it is capable of greatness.

'I joined the Communist Party, not because of wages or rent or taxation, but as a rebel in defence of human nature. I was a bit of a quixotic fellow and I began to tilt at the bloody windmills, like Sir Alfred Mond. I was given nine months' imprisonment for protesting against the harsh administration of the Means Test. I consider my imprisonment to have been a privilege. I fought an election campaign for the town council from my prison cell and failed by only a handful of votes to unseat the ex-deputy mayor, who was one of the magistrates who had sent me to prison. When I came out I got a terrific majority in Stansfield ward which was an old Conservative ward that had never been taken by either Liberals or Labour and I got it as an out-and-out left-winger; I won three elections in a row, though they tried to unseat me by putting three up and splitting the vote and all that. I went abroad as a correspondent for Kemsley Newspapers and because I couldn't attend committee meetings I resigned. There was a clash with the Communist Party, who objected to my resigning without consulting them.

'I called myself a member of the Communist Party of Great Britain, but I wasn't really an orthodox Communist. It nauseated me to do my first task as a Communist, which was to cause unrest in mills for demands for better lavatories – which of course you need, but it was urgent to think on a far grander scale than that. But the Communists said you had to get the people moving on issues they are willing to fight for; as they fight for these small issues, and meet opposition, they see where it is coming from and they learn the class war. It's sound as far as it goes, but my interests have been much wider. Because I was more interested in the aesthetic side of life, I sent a letter to the *Daily Worker* in which I said I wanted to get in touch with other men and women who were interested in founding a league for the liberation of proletarian art, writing and painting and poetry expressed through personal vision, which they were not able to do under the capitalist system of the day. They wouldn't publish it, and said it was against the rules of the Communist Party to found a united front on any issue without it coming from the top. I said, "All right, do it from the top." "No," they said. "It's useless. You can't revolutionise proletarian art until you've had the revolution. You've to wait for that." And I disagreed. I said that all this was part of the movement; there were some like myself who would fight to the death defending art and the right to express personal vision.

'I felt about the Communists as I felt about the scientists, that their ends were my beginnings. I'm interested in what comes beyond that – the inner, the real mystery, the inner mystery of it all.

'I've travelled in about forty-three countries by now. I was a guest of Mr Nehru and we had a heart-to-heart talk; and Dr Radhakrishnan before he was president invited me to dinner and I had a talk to him about East and West and that sort of thing. Not so much a political talk but more on mystical problems. I've lived with a holy man in India in his cave and discussed his views of these questions of existence. I went to the Spanish Civil War as a correspondent for Kemsley Newspapers. I also travelled in Russia, where, though I didn't actually meet Stalin, I met a lot of other Kremlin people.

'I went to Russia just after the Revolution. After arriving by sea at Leningrad we were put into a very large luxury hotel that had been converted into a hostel; there were camp beds all over the place, as many beds as they could get into one room. I'd only been there for a few hours when I heard a noise in the street. Coming from England, that was in a state of almost riotous assembly through three million unemployed, and the Means Test, my first impression was that there was a demonstration against the government – any noise or singing in the street, to me, meant a demonstration; and all our demonstrations had been anti-state. I looked out of the window and I saw a lot of people, many of them young, standing at a stopping-place for a tramcar. They were singing at the tops of their voices and they looked happy. I said to the interpreters, "Who are these people?" "They are the Sobotniki. These are the men and women who have done their week's work and are now on holiday and are going to help the farmers without pay."'

Bill put his hands to his face. He was crying.

'I can't remember them and talk about it without deep emotion. These Sobotniki were what I wanted to be and what I believed was the very heart of political Communism and they were singing and they were happy and they made me happy. But where are the Sobotniki now? That was forty years ago.'

Bill paused for a long while.

'What I despise most is meanness. My reaction to anything that's mean is to do the very opposite. I was once selling bags of coal in Todmorden when I was hard up. I hadn't any capital, and I used to order on credit a waggon-load of coal at the railway. If I could get six or seven orders I hired a horse and a man and a cart to deliver. A woman on the street there ordered two bags. I lifted the grating on the street and shot the coal down the chute and the lying swine came out and said she didn't order those bags – but she'd taken good care to see they'd gone down the chute before she said she didn't order them. My reaction – it was a bit Don Quixotic really – was to put another one down. It was bloody silly, but I gave her another bag.

'It's rather odd that I, born as a working man, should have a great admiration for true aristocratic life. At the microphone I had a long argument with C. E. M. Joad. He rather lost his temper with me in one of two broadcasts under the title "The Meaning Behind The Word". The word that we were discussing was "aristocracy". He argued that aristocracy no longer meant what it used to mean. He said that it now means a man who was either born in a certain bed or who lined his pockets successfully or who was clever at politics.

'I said, "That's not aristocracy. Even if he's been born in a certain bed if that's the way they live they cease to be aristocrats. They are declassed. Among the true aristocrats they would be kicked out – bounders, you know."

'I insisted that there is in the world and in life room for aristocracy and that I admire the aristocrat. There are some who are born natural aristocrats. I still feel that the true aristocrat can be recognised at once in the man's attitude to life and it has nothing to do with money. I have met a few and I've noticed this: that the common people recognise it when they're personally present. When the aristocrat gets up to go out, the common people open doors for him; his manners are such that they inspire from the people a response, and that is aristocracy. And there isn't a great difference between the proper craftsman and the aristocrat, you know, though socially they're wide apart. We have produced in this region proud craftsmen in all the crafts – very proud and not corrupt, generous and believers in truth and decent behaviour.

'My main art in life has been life itself. I was not dissatisfied. What I've had and what I have is good. I love it. Every bit of it. Every minute of it. So I'm not dissatisfied. But I'm unsatisfied. Unsatisfied means you like what's on the menu but there isn't enough of it.

'I've had to work for my living and when I went to see the head of the Third Programme once and I'd had terrific success broadcasting to America during the war and all over the place I said, "Aren't you interested in the outlook of a working man in the present world situation and who is articulate and has written books?" He said: "But you're not a working man," and I thought, "Well, that's a bugger! I've been working all my damned life!"'

Billy never understood why, soon after the war, he was dropped as a broadcaster. He did not perceive that his had been useful propaganda to rouse enthusiasm from a working class suspicious of the War as another duel between imperialist powers, another blood-letting like World War I to absorb a radical proletariat. Here was a working man broadcasting as belligerently as Mr Churchill himself. 'England is greater now than in Queen Elizabeth the First's day!' trumpeted the little weaver in his Yorkshire accent. But when the war was over, other broadcasters, as Billy put it 'came out of hiding in Gloucestershire and Somerset' to take over the microphone.

This friend of H. G. Wells, Bernard Shaw, Henry Williamson, Eleanor Farjeon, this 'life-long member of The Savage Club', then lived with an upper-class Bohemian artistic set in London's Marylebone High Street. It was very Bloomsbury: Blanaid O'Carrol who took her Irish maid with her to live a bohemian life; Le Comte de Vismes; and also, most importantly for Billy because of his affair with her, Lady Freda Harris, the escapee wife of Sir Percy Harris, the Liberal chief whip. Billy describes her as one who wore clothes culled from fancy dress shops, held parties at which she introduced musicians ranging from Anthony Hopkins to a 'guitar-playing waiter from Claridges', and slipped poetic billets-doux under Holt's door. ('I want to listen to you talking about the sky.') She was a lady so absorbed in her art of painting that when a barrage balloon collapsed on her studio roof, where it might have exploded, she refused admission to airforcemen, firemen and police because they would 'disturb her work'.

Billy moved into her flat. With her he met Aleister Crowley, and also went to India, she paying the expenses. He tried to sell her paintings, and she, equally unsuccessfully, his patent shuttle to the Indian government.

Billy's fame and fortune lapsed completely during the 1970s. As I knew him, he was sad, lively, humorous, idealistic, lonely, holding a cancered body together (though none of his friends suspected it) with alcohol and sheer vitality.

After his divorce in old age, he married again.

'If it happens to me, you can bet there'll be something funny about it,' he told me.

Sheila Whitley, the heiress to Whitley's brewery, wrote to him, admiring *Trigger in Europe*, and arranging for him to visit her local literary society. Before the event she came to Kilnhurst, arriving in her Rolls Royce with a picnic hamper. Whilst the chauffeur waited, these two picnicked and drank champagne on the hillside. After his visit to the literary society, Billy announced that he was to be married. 'But do you love her, Billy?' he was asked. 'No – but she listens to me,' he answered.

Their marriage lasted, if I remember rightly, about six months, and after two years of semi-separation they were divorced. Billy was irritated by her fondness for *The Archers*; by Shropshire; by his wife's 'fidgeting in bed, her restless opening and shutting of windows and so forth, and her endless dusting'.

'The bloody world's made of dust,' he remarked, one day back in Todmorden. 'We come from dust and we end in dust. Sometimes it has been very useful to me, when I used to write in it as it fell on the machines in the mill. I'm not going to get upset by a bit of dust when I have more important things to do.'

After his death, Billy was cremated. He chose a more recent lady-admirer to scatter his remains on Whirlaw, the hill that hangs above Todmorden, and she threw them into the wind, so that Billy's dust blew back into her face. It was something that seemed very typical of Billy.

5

On the day previous to my setting off from Kilnhurst there was a late spring snowstorm. The landscape was quickly obliterated. The crevices of wiry grass on the moors, that were beginning to trickle with green, disappeared.

I left with my rucksack at six o'clock the next morning. The earth was rigid with a scattering of frozen snow and little was distinguishable in the grey light, but larks were singing at a height from which they could already see the sun rising beyond the hills. The sky was absolutely clear; the stars fading into it became blue slowly. The industrial clattering of Todmorden and the Calder Valley, that had gone on all night, rang through the icy air.

I skirted the hillside above Lumbutts. Following the stream through the thin oak woods and a scattering of farms, I intended to follow the paved pack-horse road that climbs the moor which is crowned with a monument to the victory of Waterloo: Stoodley Pike. The sun had now risen high enough to colour the lip of the valley above me, whilst below remained dark. It was like a light thrust into a coal cellar. Frozen snow on the rocks glittered like eyes.

I climbed on to the rim of a plateau, the level shoulder of the hill below the moor-top. The noises of the Calder Valley were suddenly shut off. I was in a different world, one consisting of a maze of tiny, stone-walled fields. Peewits rose and tumbled in the air. Dogs at the farms started barking, one after another, before I disappeared from their view into one of those typical stony Pennine lanes with high dark walls on either side.

On these slopes is still intact (even if put to a different use) the world of the pre-nineteenth century woollen trade, of which Daniel Defoe wrote in his *A Tour Through The Whole Island of Great Britain* of 1724.

'We found the country one continued village, though mountainous every way, hardly a house standing out of speaking distance from another, and the day clearing up, and the sun shining, we could see that at almost every house there was a tenter, and almost on every tenter a piece of cloth . . . whenever we passed any house we found a little rill or gutter of running water . . . and at every considerable house was a manufactory or work-house, and as they could not do their business without water, the little streams were so parted and guided by gutters or pipes, and by turning and dividing the streams, that none of these houses were without a river . . . running into and through their workhouses. . . . Amongst the manufacturers' houses are likewise scattered an infinite number of cottages or small dwellings, in which dwell the workmen which are employed, the women and children of whom are always busy carding, spinning so that no hands being unemployed, all can gain their bread, even

PREVIOUS PAGE. Todmorden. 'Road, railway, river and canal are plaited in the sump of a valley where the dark towns of Lancashire and Yorkshire intermingle like the threads of spun cotton or wool.'

from the youngest to the ancient; hardly anything above four years old, but its hands are sufficient to it self.'

The 'tenters' were the wooden frames, fitted with rows of metal hooks, upon which the new cloth was stretched so that it would dry without shrinking – the phrase 'on tenterhooks' comes from this practice. There are still places called 'Tenter Fields': there is one east of Halifax, for instance. These fields, as shown in old depictions of the district, must have been some of the most striking characteristics of the Calder Valley, especially the large acreages next to the big industrial mills.

The western Pennines might also be described as an oat-culture, for that is what they lived on, growing their crop in these small enclosures which are now entirely given over to grass. The staple food was oat-cakes, or havercake – a mixture of oatmeal and water, with added to it salt and yeast, that was heated on a bakestone and then hung to dry on strings above the fireplace – which must have been a typical sight in moorland kitchens until the First World War. Because of these oat-cakes a local regiment was called 'The Havercake Lads' (during the Napoleonic Wars it was famous as the Duke of Wellington's), a title going back to the Civil War when Godfrey Bosvile of Gunthwaite House raised one thousand West Yorkshire men, all of them over six feet tall – supposedly from eating havercakes. Oats fed the horses, too, and I have heard it said that you can still recognise a Calder Valley-bred pony because it will digest oat straw. For more palatable human consumption, oat-cakes could be mixed with blood to make blood puddings.

My road broke at last onto the open moor again, and before me was a long line of paving stones reaching up the hill: a pack-horse route to Lancashire. The shaping of stone, whether by masons or by the wear of humans, animals or weather, always stirs me. Here, every paving stone had been worn into a saddle-shaped trough by the passage of horses and men. It is the same shaping that one sees in the stones of mill stairs, and it always moves me to think of the working men, women and children whose feet sculpted these shapes, the only memorials to a hundred years of daily labour. Yet when mills and passageways are demolished, they are broken or thrown away.

Near the causeway are the foundations of an engineered road, leading nowhere, but cutting up the hill; a reminder of John Fielden. Rather than ignore or give charity to men thrown out of work due to the failure of raw cotton to reach Lancashire during the American Civil War, Fielden gave them some pride by having them build this, later abandoned, road.

So I climbed up to the Stoodley Pike monument. There are more hills crowned with phallic spikes in the mid-Pennines than in any region of England, perhaps of the world; part of the striving phallicism of chimneys, church towers, spiked railings, steep gables and mill-gates that everywhere proclaims the nature of the Industrial Revolution. Stoodley Pike Monument, which is the height of a three-storey building, is black, lugubrious, Egyptian-looking, and funereal rather than joyous.

Architecturally its achievement is no more than to destroy the scale of the hills from wherever it is visible, which is for miles around.

However, one of its great tomb-like recesses now sheltered me from the icy wind. Then I clambered down the slopes of Erringden Moor, making for Hebden Bridge.

Larks singing over the thawing slopes; and a tiny flowering rush, yellow with pollen in the snow.

Hebden Bridge is a place of bookshops, antique shops and restaurants, all open on Sundays. In other words, a tourist town – love it or hate it. A mill town once, its main industries the manufacture of trousers and corduroy, it was discovered during the early 1970s by those whom the locals were soon calling 'hippies'.

My own theory, having lived briefly in the town during the pre-invasion year, is that this discovery had something to do with the fare-staging of British Rail. I forget the exact prices now; but on the track between Manchester and Leeds, Hebden Bridge was a fare stage beyond which the price increased disproportionately. The town is also dramatically beautiful to approach by train. Both of these reasons made it attractive to people growing claustrophobic in the bed-sit squats overflowing around the universities and colleges of Manchester and Leeds. 'Hippies', poor but intellectually adventurous, moved into cheap terraced houses. After them came more of their kind and of what catered for them: bookshops that stocked poetry, craft shops, 'junk' shops that have steadily moved up-market for a changing clientele as the dying town of Hebden Bridge turned into an 'exciting' place to live: a Yorkshire Islington. However much the 'hippies' were scorned, trade boomed because of them. All ideas were represented in Hebden Bridge, from socialism at the Trades Club, suddenly come alive with pop and theatre groups, to the headquarters of a matriarchal group, 'Lux Madriana', at Macpelah House. (They have now moved to western Ireland.)

It was one cosy place to be if there was anything freaky about you; one place to find sisterhood or brotherhood if you were battered in the sexual stakes; one town in West Yorkshire that was alive on Sundays, where books, poetry and music might be discussed in the pubs.

Hebden Bridge is an extreme example of the change that has taken place in all the smaller villages and hamlets. After the Second World War, when the economic pulse of the textile industry throbbed so low that it almost ceased, the only thing that saved such places was a new, often unlikeable gentrification. It has been unlikeable when it has shown too little respect for the architectural quality, the architectural unity and the craftsmanship of what it has taken over.

Yes, those pretty little hamlets of the Pennines are monuments to the misery of an exploited class. Their damp overcrowding in a time of plenty, a plenty which their inhabitants actually created, is a disgrace to our history; the webs of stone ginnels and snickets (local words for passageways), and the stairways passing from them down the

Stoodley Pike Monument. '. . . part of the striving phallicism . . . that everywhere proclaims the patriarchal nature of the Industrial Revolution.'

fields to connect with the factories, draw upon the land the map of that slavery. But in the end, the only things created by those lives were stone houses, walls, mills and stairways, with an unrepeatable, or at any rate unrepeated, craftsmanship, and it is an insult to their memory to demolish all in the belief that we are thereby ridding ourselves of an oppression, or of nothing better than the reminders of oppression, although this is the justification for demolition expressed in many a council chamber.

The new inhabitants of the villages must be credited with this: they have saved, even though in a gentrified form, what would otherwise certainly have disappeared.

For them, a region whose most basic character is one of remoteness, hardness, labour and struggle, has become a country playground little more than half an hour's drive on a motorway from Manchester or Leeds. Almost no-one on the Pennines is now a spinner, weaver or textile engineer, and few of them are farmers. They are salespeople and technocrats from the city; people in the media, the arts, public relations, advertising; they are representatives or information-providers, people from all the new urban professions which have no connection with the Pennine region or its history, its natural environment or resources. Therefore they are apt to disregard the architectural unity which came naturally to the original creators of the villages.

Cars are not merely a convenience, they are the very lifeblood of the new villager, and the need to park or to garage them is the cause of the first and most conspicuous offence. In these most compact of villages, among whose most refined features are the spatial relationships between small doors, windows and passageways, relatively huge garage entrances are contrived out of what were cellars and kitchens.

The disappearance of coal as the major fuel has brought about another ubiquitous ugliness. Chimneys were once an integral part of cottage architecture. What happens to them now? People generally care about the appearance of their front door, but not many think of what happens on their roof. Yet in the Pennines you are generally looking over roofs – someone else's roof, where the builder, unsupervised on the top of the house, has crudely cemented up a chimney, taken away the chimney pots and used the flue for a protruding, plastic ventilator pipe; has made, in fact, a mess of it.

Indoor bathrooms are another unoriginal Pennine feature. Their introduction has led to snakings of plastic pipes over the stone walls. Picture windows, telephone lines, television aerials . . . cement lintels replacing stone ones . . . paved footpaths and snickets obstructed or dug up because of the desire for a little garden . . . upon the public footpaths, geraniums sprouting out of the tops of those fallen chimney-pots.

It is for such incongruous and sickly-sweet dreams that our Pennine villages have been saved. But saved they have been, whilst the major towns, Huddersfield, Bradford, Halifax, Rochdale, Oldham, exhibit their decay.

From Hebden Bridge I climbed to Heptonstall, following the route from the old bridge.

Hebden Bridge. 'Yellow stone set in yellow-green moorland, at the edge of woodland.'

A good way to make anyone fall in love with a West Yorkshire town is to show them the views of Hebden Bridge looking back from this packhorse track. There is some lovely Victorian architecture to be seen, especially the school at Birchcliffe, its yellow stone set in yellow-green moorland at the end of the woodlands of Hardcastle Crags.

Heptonstall was once, in pre-industrial times, a rich cloth-town. Its heavy stones cluster on the hill-top like a medieval fortress, and it seems hardly to have a blade of grass. It is the size of a small village, but by the quality of the masonry and of the architecture you can tell that it was once the home of wealthy merchants and prosperous artisans. Its beauty is brooding and melancholic. It is like that in decay, and in its romantic revival as a tourist attraction; I suspect it was the same when it was new, or in its heyday.

Especially in keeping with this, right at the heart of the village, are the blackened ruins of the collapsed medieval church of St Thomas à Becket, whose great stone roof was blown off in a nineteenth-century gale. Here, also, is the grave of Sylvia Plath, the American poet, with a path kept open to it by the feet of the curious or idolising students at the nearby school of creative writing at Lumb Bank. Heptonstall, a place which was almost as neglected as Mill Bank when I first came here (the local people having deserted for the adjacent housing estate), is now proudly laid out with walk-trails that offer the keys to its history; details and items of which are nicely represented in the museum made out of the old grammar school. If you can get the vicar to let you climb the church tower, as I have done, one of the most dramatic views in Yorkshire will be revealed. Heptonstall shows itself as like an Italian hill-town, with the great chasms of the woods falling away from it.

Through Heptonstall the road follows the spine of the hill, breaking out onto the view again a mile further on at Slack Bottom, and Slack. At Slack the way divides, on either side of the Baptist Chapel, into two of the most beautiful lanes across the Pennines. On the right is the route through Widdop to Nelson, and on the left is the Long Causeway, above the valley to Burnley.

The latter is redolent of a very ancient past indeed. Perhaps this is because it passes by Bride Stones: soon on your left hand you see the amazing site of a great ball of stone, like a pregnant stomach, balanced on a slender stem, and in a short while other boulders tumbled about the roadside like giants' playthings. Perhaps it is because, at the other end of it before it tumbles into Burnley, the nubs of the hills hold so many tumuli, cairns, iron-age enclosures, burial mounds and stone circles – around the end of this road there are nine monuments of this kind, their backs to the hills, and looking over the broad valley beyond.

I was not going as far as that, but planned to cut across woods and moorlands on my right, to reach Haworth. I stood at *Slack Bottom* and savoured the candidness, the straightforward honesty and humour of the names of the hills around. *Back of Behind. Cold Soil. Pisser Clough. Too To Hill.* Other names tell of what was done or happened there. *Rush Candle Clough. Flaight Clough* and *Flaight Hill. (Flaight* is a

Heptonstall. 'The blackened ruins of the collapsed medieval church of St Thomas à Becket.'

ghost, and a *clough* is a valley.) And what about *Idle*, and *The Idle Working Men's Club*, in Bradford? Or *Friendly* in Halifax? *Bottom O'T'Moor, Foul Syke* and *Grand View*? Try upon your tongue *Luddenden*, or *Staups*, giving full slow value to every consonant and vowel, as you should, and automatically their poetry will draw you into speaking in the rich Yorkshire way.

Reservoirs are scattered over the moorland, and they too have their history. Take for example the Walshaw Dean reservoir, along the grim bank of which I had to walk in order to cross the moor to Haworth. These were built by one Enoch Tempest, born the son of a quarry-owner in Haworth in 1843. The liquid element and the watery storms conjured by his name haunted even his youth. The liquid then was ale, and the storms were those of his notorious drunkenness, that, it is recorded, frightened the villagers. After one spree he awoke in New York, not knowing how he had got there; apparently it was having to work his passage home that sobered him up for good. Back in Yorkshire he became the famous teetotal builder of reservoirs. The secret of his success was that he made use, in the most unlikely places, of the new steam-locomotives. His engines, Minnie, Harold, Annie, Little Egret, Tenacity and Esau, conquered the moors.

He first built a reservoir near Keighley and then one near Matlock. He widened the canal in Leicester. Then he built Clough Bottom reservoir at Windy Bank, 1,000 feet high on the Burnley Road, followed by Barley Reservoir, below Pendle Hill near Nelson. He was now rich, and moved to live in luxury at Oak Dene near Marple, Cheshire.

In 1900 he submitted his tender to Halifax Corporation for building a chain of three reservoirs at Walshaw Dean. The site is 1,000 feet above sea-level. He erected wooden huts at Heptonstall to house Irish navvies; a settlement that came to be called Dawson City. From here he built a three-foot gauge railway which ran for five miles to the reservoir sites. Part of the engineering for this was a trestle viaduct made of pitch pine, 700 feet long, 105 feet above the stream at Blakedean. (The bases of the trestles are still standing.) Tempest's success came through his audacity in building tracks across the bogs and through his ingenuity in getting engines and rolling stock to that elevation in the first place. Fifteen locomotives were dragged from Hebden Bridge station over several Saturday afternoons, a time when the cart-horses of tradesmen could be hired to make up the teams of up to sixteen horses that helped steam-lorries drag the locomotives 400 feet up the hill to the workshops at Dawson City. Horse-tramcars from Liverpool were converted to become the 'Paddy Mail' that took the Irish navvies from Dawson City to the reservoirs at half-past five every morning.

Poor Enoch Tempest; a storm of excess in ambition, audacity and imagination! After he had built his reservoirs, they leaked (due only to the contemporary lack of knowledge of geology), and the shock of losing all his money in trying to repair them, in accordance with his contract, brought on a stroke. He died in 1908.

But in one of a bleak terrace of a dozen houses, flush to the road on the hill ridge at Colden beyond Heptonstall, lives Charles Chambers, who was the driver of Esau, one of the engines. He is ninety-five years of age, yet he walks sturdily. His face is long, large and cadaverous.

He wore the jacket and trousers of an old-fashioned engine driver. 'A come up here eighteen year ago to wear me old clothes out!' he shouted. '*Am still here!*' he added, raising his voice further, as if challenging me to dispute it.

The house is clean and tidy. On the wall over the kitchen fireplace he is painting a picture. It is a picture of the view through the kitchen window. The artist is evidently short-sighted; but there is Stoodley Pike, and there is the field of rushes below his window falling to the lip of the Calder Valley that lies between here and Stoodley. He has made the monument by cutting it out of plywood and glueing it on. He was creating this view when I visited him a year ago, and layers of paint have been applied since.

'I've still got all them walls to do!' he shouted.

On the pot-cupboard is a smaller picture, of Esau, very tiny but in full detail, crossing the equally detailed viaduct.

Charles Chambers walked into the room at the front, that is to the other side of the house facing the road, and paused before the window there as if it was to be the inspiration for another picture. But what brought him delight was the sight of his garden, which was about the size of two graves and built into the bank on the other side of the road. Its wooden fence, a foot high, and its gate of the same height, were thickly painted in cream, brick red, and dark green – the same colours, indeed the same pigments, as in his mural paintings. In it, the pebbled paths, eight inches wide, were lined with clipped bushes a few inches high. They led to a village church, cottages and pub built out of plywood, divided also by tiny pebble-stone steps. In the corner of the garden a five-foot high pole carried a little windmill that whirred and twisted in the moorland wind. In the centre of the garden was a plaque: 'What will our harvest be.'

There was no question mark, I noticed. It was not a question, but a rhetorical statement, for Charles Chambers belonged still to the age of certainty, like Enoch Tempest and the other builders of reservoirs, and all the other Yorkshire builders.

Past the reservoirs, then, to climb over a fresh block of moorlands, along the Pennine Way by Withens Height to a view of Haworth and of the Keighley Valley. I have broken onto the hills that were loved by Emily Brontë; also by *E. Wilkinson. A Rambler. Died August 31 1964 aged 75* (according to his or her memorial on a pathside cairn.) Top Withens, a derelict huddle of stones in a boggy trough, is the assumed site of *Wuthering Heights*. Further down is that lovely moorland spot known as the Brontë Waterfall. Enshaw Knoll, a name to make you think of Emily, is on the right.

Then Haworth town closes tight around me, as is the manner of the hill towns, with glimpses down snickets, of the hills, of an industrial valley, and of the railway which was celebrated, even before it was built, in Bill o'Th'Hoylus End's *History o' the Haworth Railway Fro' Th' Beginning to th' End, wi' an account of the opening Surremuny.*

Wi persperashun on his brow,
He says good folks I'll tell you now,
Oud Blu Beard's nasty wizened cow
Has swallowed plan o'th'railway . . .

He said me blood begins to boil,
To think at we should work and toil
An even th' cattle cannot thoyle
Ta let us have a railway.

On hearing this the Haworth folk
Began to think it were no joke
And wished at greedy cow may choke,
At swallowed th' plan o' th' railway . . .

The narrow streets of Haworth would be as stonily quiet as Heptonstall if it were not for that steam railway, which became famous as the setting of *The Railway Children*; and for the Brontë sisters whose secretive lives and fantasies, grown in the gloom and quiet of a northern vicarage, have resulted in their native village street becoming as noisy as London's Oxford Street. There are the Brontë Tweedmill, Brontë cafés, Heathcliff Café, Haworth Rock, and a pub outside town where you can buy a warmed-up hamburger called a Brontë Sandwich. In the museum (an extension of the parsonage where the Brontë family, so the curator informed me, 'wrote good, clean, imaginative love stories') are cases holding the minutiae of nineteenth-century spinsters' lives. A bonnet and a wreath that may have held Charlotte's veil in place; Charlotte's mittens, boots and work basket; the hat 'said to have been worn by Ellen Nussey at Charlotte's wedding'; Anne's 'small box'; a pin-cushion said to have belonged to Ellen Nussey; a smelling-salts bottle; a nail brush; and 'THE ACTUAL TRUNK' that Charlotte bought in Brussels. Objects as sad, delicate and faded as pinned-out moths.

6

In Haworth you can at most times fall upon an open café, a shop selling snacks, and a bed for the night; things not always to be relied upon hereabouts.

These basics satisfied, it interested me most to pass through the graveyard. This was not entirely because it seemed the most appropriate place to rest with a stomach full of chips, grease and processed peas. The Haworth churchyard, surrounding (incidentally) a church much 'developed' according to late Victorian taste after the demise of the Brontës, is famous and much-photographed for its packed and weighty graves, which express even to the most ignorant and unperceptive eye the charismatic presence of Death in past times. The visitor here realises that families like the youthful Brontës, thinned or entirely felled by Death, were not a unique or even an unusual phenomenon. Not only were such mortal illnesses as tuberculosis commonplace; Haworth and other Pennine communities suffered periodic visitations (perhaps every three or four years) of typhus, a decimation which they called 'the plague'.

Mrs Gaskell, Charlotte Brontë's biographer, was shocked by Haworth's atmosphere of despair. 'The passing and funeral bells so frequently tolling, and filling the air with mournful sound, and, when they are still, the "chip chip" of the mason as he cut the gravestones in a shed close by' struck her as the typical sounds of the town.

Where Death is fearful, Religion flourishes. On the far side of that potent graveyard, beyond an iron gate, there crosses the meadows, climbing up the hill, a path made of well-cut paving stones, close-fitting and end-to-end like a ladder to Heaven. Follow it at right angles around a field wall. It will lead you after half a mile to an old farmhouse, Sowdens. It is long, low, with one end sunk into the fields, and (to put it mildly, and I hope not rudely) lacking any pretensions to smartness; a working hill farm, with machinery, straw, animals and poultry scattered around it. The main entrance is now on the longest wall of the house; but at the far, and lower, end is a massive stone porch, with a great oak door, quite outdoing in grandeur anything else at Sowdens.

It is a porch associated with a certain past owner, and its powerful massiveness accords with his temperament. He indeed was surrogate king over Death. At Sowdens, take a look at that porch, and the stone pathway that he built for himself, his family and servants trailing behind him, to reach Haworth Church. The Methodist Parson William Grimshaw; 'Mad Grimshaw'.

Before the Brontës and the steam railway, it was Grimshaw's Methodism that made Haworth famous, and his parsonage that was visited. He was the Wesleys' lieutenant in the north, and was chosen to be their national successor, but he died first.

As Mad Grimshaw's eighteenth-century biographer John Newton put it:

'Haworth is one of those obscure places, which, like the fishing towns in Galilee favoured with our Lord's presence, owe all their celebrity to the Gospel. The name of Haworth would scarcely be known at a distance, were it not connected with the name of Grimshaw. The bleak and barren face of the adjacent country was no improper emblem of the state of the inhabitants; who in general had little more sense of religion than their cattle, and were wild and uncultivated like the rocks and mountains which surrounded them. But, by the blessing of God upon Mr Grimshaw's ministry, this desert soon became a fruitful field, a garden of the Lord, producing many trees of righteousness . . . and the barren wilderness rejoiced and blossomed like the rose. As in ancient times the whole congregation have been often seen in tears on account of their provocations against God.'

'A few such as he would make a nation tremble. He carries fire wherever he goes,' John Wesley wrote of this powerful orator.

He had need of fire in Haworth. John Wesley, who addressed the common people of every parish of the country, thought West Yorkshire the most savage and barbarous region that he ever visited. (It was also his favourite, because of this. 'That place suits me best, where so many are groaning for redemption', he wrote.)

Haworth's Pennine savagery, and Grimshaw's inability finally to do anything more than merely suppress it, is best illustrated by what happened after he died. The Rev. Mr Redhead, Grimshaw's successor, could not even control his parish church for as long as three weeks. At the reading of the lesson during his first service the whole congregation, clattering their heavy wooden clogs as loudly as possible, left the church. The following Sunday a half-wit seated on the back of an ass, his face towards its tail and with a pile of old hats upon his head, was driven around the aisles. On the third Sunday a drunken and soot-covered chimney-sweep climbed the pulpit steps and embraced the clergyman. Mr Redhead was chased into the yard, covered with the contents of the soot bag, and finally pursued into the public house, The Black Bull. It says a lot for Patrick Brontë that he could follow this event; and even more for William Grimshaw that he could earlier have tamed these people into church-going and Wesleyanism.

Wesleyanism gained its power because it offered, during life itself, the key to what happened after death – no need to wait for Judgement until you met your Maker. The vision of eternity, whether it be damned or golden, appeared for the Methodist in a moment of instant revelation; and if damned, you could still, later, in the same instantaneous manner, know yourself redeemed.

William Grimshaw was an especially effective Wesleyan for two main reasons. First of all because of his energy, which was enormous. In 1743, he started twelve meetings for prayer and worship in cottages scattered distantly over the intractable moorlands of his parish. As people here often could not travel to church (or said that they couldn't), he went to their cottages, or if that was impossible, then sent his sermons to be read there. In bad or good weather he walked or travelled by horse over

Haworth Parsonage. '. . . secretive lives and fantasies, grown in the gloom and quiet of a northern vicarage.'

the moors, preaching twelve to fourteen times in what he called a 'lazy week' and twenty to thirty times in a busy one. That was only a start. Later on, adding devotion to Methodism to his duties as an Anglican clergyman (Methodism remained a society within the Church until after Wesley's death) he travelled, with the stamina usually regarded as a unique characteristic of John Wesley himself, over the whole north of England.

The second reason for Grimshaw's effectiveness was the single-mindedness of his 'vision' (if we may call it that). He was a man driven by, amongst other things, sexual loneliness following the death of his first wife Sarah. After she died there came a total inversion of his character, from loving to damning, from happy-go-lucky to measuring the moment of doom, and from cheerfulness to deep private melancholy. Though he married again it was evidently loveless, and in any case his second wife also died early, in a Haworth 'plague'. Grimshaw remained haunted, confessing in his diary to, amongst other temptations, those of masturbation. His only escape was through his work. He tackled God's mission with the practicality typical of those whom he chose to be his parish clerks, his friends and neighbours – that is, of an ambitious Yorkshire trader or artisan – keeping a ledger of his debit and credit with God, balancing his books (sins against good works), daily, weekly, monthly, yearly; making his friendships with fellow Methodists, tradesmen and sensible master-clothiers; enclosing the moor to make grazing for the horses of visiting preachers; and investing in the new turnpike roads because they helped his work of itinerant salvation as well as trade. Yes, indeed, a practical man.

He was notorious for circulating Haworth whilst the psalm was being chanted before the sermon (psalm 119 was his favourite for this purpose, it being the longest) to drive malingering parishioners into church with a horse-whip. There they learned Grimshaw's version of Hell. The saved in Heaven had their pleasures increased by being in sight of Hell, even though it might be their own loved ones who were burning; and such sins as whistling, singing, dancing, or even failing to reprove a neighbour for those things, was sufficient to consign one to the flames.

'How many communicants did you find on coming to Haworth?' the Archbishop of York asked, during an enquiry on Mad Grimshaw (as he had come to be called) for having attended the Methodist Conference in Leeds in 1749.

'Twelve, my lord.'

'How many have you now?'

'In winter between three and four hundred, according to the weather. In summer nearer 1,200.'

'We can find no fault in Mr Grimshaw,' said the Archbishop, 'seeing he is instrumental in bringing so many to the Lord's Table.'

There were occasions later when 6,000 people came to hear Charles Wesley preach in Haworth. I have a suspicion that the roots of the Yorkshire and Lancashire love of walking and hiking began with people clambering over the moors to these meetings.

The Rev.ᵈ W.ᵐ Grimshaw: B.A.
of Christ's Coll. Cambridge.

Late Minister of Haworth Yorkshire.

Rev. William Grimshaw, of Haworth. 'A few such as he would make a nation
tremble. He carries fire wherever he goes.' (John Wesley)

'Members of Darney's new formed societies at Millers Barn, and at other places, used to walk twenty miles to attend the ministries of Grimshaw at Haworth. Their route was . . . over hills, some of which were 1,000 feet above sea-level, across deep and rugged valleys; but their new-born zeal surmounted all difficulties,' wrote J. W. Laycock in his *Methodist Heroes of the Great Haworth Round* of 1909.

'*What hath God wrought in the midst of these rough mountains!*' exclaimed John Wesley.

After his death ('I have nothing to do but step out of my bed into Heaven. I have my foot on its threshold already.') Grimshaw, as he had arranged on Sarah's death many years earlier, was buried side by side with her in Luddenden, his body carried by horse litter fourteen miles over the moors to her. It was probably in order to remain in the vicinity of her grave that this man, whose abilities could easily have made him a national leader of Methodism, which at that time meant being a leader in national life, stayed in Haworth.

It is a love story, then, but a curious and perverse one. Grimshaw is a man who dammed up his love, his inner feminine promptings, to become self-consuming, self- destroying, finding escape but not release in the masculine activity of promoting his patriarchal God. Who was also the God of the new industry, that was likewise turning a deaf ear to the feminine influences of the land and of Nature, in order to exploit Her.

Methodism, mill-ownership, and the new industrial wealth went hand in hand. 'Methodists in every place grow diligent and frugal, consequently they increase in goods,' wrote John Wesley; and K. S. Inglis points out in his *Churches and The Working Class in Victorian England*: 'In 1856 the historian of a flourishing Methodist circuit declared that many a rich man would have been still in squalid poverty if Methodism had not taken him by the hand. It was she that saved him from rags – put him on his feet – gave him a character, and placed him in the path of industry in which he has found both affluence and position.'

Religion generally makes a virtue of poverty. But in West Yorkshire in the nineteenth century, when it could be seen that many were making large fortunes quickly, it appeared that the way to become as they were was to do as they did – that is, to attend chapel. As a power in the Western world, this Methodist legacy is now more alive than ever: take, for example, the contemporary evangelical preacher Mr Jerry Falwell, who, according to the *Sunday Times* of 3 March 1985, said, 'Material wealth is God's way of blessing people who put Him first.' The same report quotes *Good Housekeeping*'s claim that Falwell is 'the second most admired man in America'.

In late eighteenth-century Yorkshire, before money was raised to build chapels, cottages and barns were adapted, and farm kitchens, like those at Hardibutts Farm

Octagonal, eighteenth-century 'preaching house' designed by John Wesley, in Heptonstall. 'God's mansion . . . as bleak as an outcrop of millstone grit . . . as harsh, spiritually, as the mills were, physically.'

and at Cross Ends Farm, in Crimsworth Dean above Hebden Bridge, were opened for services. In time there came a fury of building, when the Methodists (especially the Methodists, but other denominations too) littered the hillsides with great chapels. God's mansion, as it turned out, was as bleak as an outcrop of millstone grit; its conditions were as harsh spiritually, as the the mills were physically. The forbidding elements in its doctrine were reflected in the forbidding appearance of its buildings. They were churches without steeples and which rarely carried even a cross, let alone any sculpture, because these were marks of Anglican, Papist or pagan idolatry. Instead they were decorated with abstract patterns and arabesques, or with the texts 'God is love' and 'Repent ye for The Kingdom of Heaven is at Hand', with a clock, a high pew for the preachers or officers, and a glass of water. Later they grew into glorious edifices: eclectic buildings in all the fashionable styles of the late nineteenth century – neo-classic, Gothic, or Art Nouveau; they smelled of pine, varnish and wax polish. How many children grew up feeling that chapel contained the appearance and flavour of Heaven itself, as they sang the comically banal hymns of Stevens or Sankey!

Bear with me when I say the crime is great
Of those who practise coming late;
As if God's services were far too long,
So they omit the opening prayer or song.

A little less indulgence in the bed –
A little more contrivance in the head –
A little more devotion in the mind
Would quite prevent your being so behind.

Some of the hymns were the epitome of the busy Methodist tradesman:

I would like to die, said Willie, if my papa could die too.
But he says he isn't ready, 'cos he's got so much to do . . .

and some could be bent to the sauciness of the mill-girl:

Oh for a man . . .
oh for a man . . .
oh for a man . . .
sion in the sky!

Our society, which is diligently re-converting mills and railways to museums of their former state, has not (as far as I know) restored any of the chapels to their former appearance. A clutch of surviving worshippers have kept some Calder Valley chapels to their intended function, by bussing across the hills to different chapels every Sunday, to air them with hymns and psalms. The rot has also reached down into the more deeply-founded Church of England; at Cotton Stones church, near Mill Bank, the elderly worshippers praise their God and keep themselves warm within a polythene tent erected in the nave.

All the non-conformist chapels are either semi-derelict, or are converted to other purposes; usually homes for atheists. The chapel ethos of the villages has evaporated before the sun of a brand of materialism that feels it is its own justification and doesn't need God to underwrite it; a society that takes its models from *Dallas* and other TV soap operas, not from Mr Grimshaw's lurid oratory.

It is not perhaps as guiltless as it imagines itself to be, for in a sense nothing changes. The same demons haunt Homer's *Odyssey*, the gargoyles of medieval churches, the monsters of science fiction and popular video films. As I witness the new Yorkshire villagers gathering to watch films in pubs or in their neighbours' houses, enjoying frissons from heroic martyrdoms or sacrifices, diabolical invaders from other planets, and Good conquering Evil (which is the staple form of cops-and-robbers stories), I feel that we have not travelled very far from the thrills of Mr Grimshaw's chapel. As to be human is to be limited, but also to possess a soul that gives gleams and glimpses of perfection, there will always be a need of balm for troubled psyches; there will always be those, whether in the business of religion or that of trying to make a worldly living, who will provide and profit from it.

So where, then, is one to look for examples of these chapels that show something of the glory they once had?

The finest one I can think of in the Calder Valley is Birchcliffe Chapel in Hebden Bridge. Now turned into a nest of offices for the Rowntree Trust, it still shows all the glorious intentions of those who built it to commemorate the great early Baptist, Dan Taylor. Taylor was a local man of the eighteenth century, who began working in a Halifax coal pit at the age of five, but 'heard the word' in adolescence and became a Baptist. Whilst running a farm-shop and preaching fanatically, he also found the time to quarry the stone and build the first Hebden Bridge chapel with his own hands.

There is a chapel on Sowerby Lane, Boulder Clough, near Sowerby, which has a grand interior. Whatever one thinks of the aesthetics of the carpentry, the craftsmanship is wonderful, and now in the process of being dismantled; the great rail and pulpit of this chapel, the God of which might have been named 'Temperance', has I believe been sold to make a bar in California! On Steep Lane, nearby, there is a chapel still used by the Methodists, and which still seems awesome with their grim power.

In these chapels, and even outside them, in the fields, the factories, and in homes, there once took place frenzies of religious 'conversion'. Adults embarrassed by their suddenly discovered guilt and sin before their watching children, 'cried to the Lord to save their souls'. One preacher, Isaac Marsden, drew a chalk line across the floor of

Mount Tabor Chapel, Halifax, and invited his congregation either to step over the line into eternal life, or 'to remain for ever in outer darkness and alone'. A man shouted to his daughter, 'Come on, Nellie, help me sing, I'm on my way to glory where pleasures never die!' A nailmaker, Jim Melling, was converted whilst he stood on a chair at home. He shouted, 'I am son of a King!' and his mother asked if he'd gone out of his mind. 'No,' he replied, 'I'm coming back to it.'

John Turton lived in Horbury and played the fiddle. When he became 'convicted of sin' he decided that his violin was 'a snare of the Devil that bewitched and threatened to destroy him' and that it 'came between him and salvation'. One night, walking the road between Horbury and Dirtcar, he turned the question over in his mind: 'Shall it be the fiddle, the public house and the Devil; or Christ, the Chapel and salvation?' He saw a flash from a fire of thorns in a field, and this seemed to be a sign from God. He jumped the hedge and thrust his fiddle into the fire.

The nation that had won the Battle of Waterloo and was also conquering nature so dramatically, particularly in Lancashire and West Yorkshire, saw military analogies in these victories over sin. 'Every night, during the crusade, that tiny room became alive with the power of God, as Jim Beesley stormed the gates of Heaven in prayer,' is typical of the way in which Methodists expressed themselves.

Foreign enemies, undisciplined nature, and the inner life of man were all conquered and tamed in that century.

Give me the faith which can remove
And sink the mountain to the plain

was Charles Wesley's expression of that relationship between the Methodist faith and the subjugation of nature.

The power and aura of nineteenth-century preachers was as that of pop singers today. The huge meetings held in such places as Haworth churchyard, and to which crowds travelled for miles, were like modern open-air festivals, with rhetoric and hymns in place of lyrics and chords. In 1899, the Rev. J. Baker Norton described in the *Methodist Magazine* one of these 'outpourings of the spirit':

'Men could not settle to work and it was no unusual thing for the miners, in the bowels of the earth, to lay aside their tools in order that they might hold prayer meetings . . . Down in the gloom, Heaven's light shone in upon penitent hearts and they became new creatures . . . In many of the houses and mills the hymns heard in the services were sung daily.'

Wedding at the Salvation Army Citadel, Halifax. 'Shall it be the fiddle, the public house and the Devil; or Christ, the Chapel and Salvation?'

7

My route from Haworth is through Oxenhope and over the moors via Cold Edge, to pick up the first stirrings out of the peat of Luddenden Brook, and then down the long wooded valley by the waterfalls of Luddenden Dean to Luddenden itself. This is approximately the route that would have been followed by Grimshaw's funeral procession. It is also the way often travelled by Branwell Brontë between home and his ill-tended duties as station-master at Luddenden Foot, where his passion was more for leaving the station in the charge of his colleague and rambling the moors and the Dean in the company of a member of the Luddenden Reading Society.

They used to meet in the Lord Nelson pub, and when I first went there, in about 1960, the landlord showed me where the books had been kept. It was a mahogany box, about three feet long, its proportions and whole appearance that of a child's coffin. The craftsmanship with which it was made, probably by one of the members, speaks of its importance to their lives. The subscribers ranged from being the owners of mills and fine houses, to William Heaton, a handloom weaver who taught himself to read and write by studying the tombstones in the churchyard. He wrote an autobiography which gives an account of the flora and fauna of the Dean, and he also left a description of Branwell Brontë: 'I shall never forget his love for the sublime and beautiful works of nature, and I have heard him dilate on the sweet strains of the nightingale.'

An example not only of Heaton's own literary style, I feel, but also of the way they talked in the Lord Nelson; where, convivial as they might all be, 'drunkenness, swearing, or any other kind of bad language' brought a fine of twopence. On the one hand, there was the classicism of William Dearden, 'the bard of Caldene' (Calderdale), who conducted his courtship, amongst the rising mills and the newly-besmirched moors, in Greek and Latin. And on the other hand there was the demonism of Branwell Brontë, and especially of his friend the sculptor Joseph Leyland who was inspired by those same 'Greek marbles' which Christopher Rawson brought back to Yorkshire, to manufacture colossal, overwrought sculptures of heroic figures, Heracles, Spartacus, Satan (Milton's Satan), etc; all of which were disaster-prone, for they either dropped apart during the casting or fell off the cart that was taking them to exhibition.

PREVIOUS PAGE. Murgatroyd's Mill and the parish graveyard at Luddenden. 'The people who still dominate this area of the Pennines are the practical ninteenth-century men and women who once made the Industrial Revolution of steam, coal, machinery, engineering and textiles.'

We laugh at these failed heroic and romantic postures, so typical of any Yorkshire self-help poets' or philosophers' club; yet in their narrow confined world these people had to face, in their personal working lives, the transformation of a society.

One of the most poignant memorials to this transformation is above Luddenden Dean, at Saltonstall; poignant because it is so modest and discreet. Overlooking that hillside is a tiny, isolated Methodists' graveyard and within it the grave of children who must have seen nothing of the beauty of this place; or if they did so it would have been no more than heart-rending glimpses from their imprisonment:

In Memory of Orphans employed by I & I. C. Calvert, Wainstalls.
Mary Ellen Clark, aged 14 years.
Alice Devitt, aged 12 years.
Elizabeth Edwards, aged 17 years.
John Johnson, aged 12 years.
Sarah Shaw, died May 17th 1892 aged 15 years.
Anne Larrings, died March 7th 1895 aged 16 years.
Mary Emery, died Jan. 27th 1895 aged 15 years.

All of them buried in the one grave, near the roadside, no doubt not having chosen to be remembered as Methodists, and given for memorial a plain and mechanical job by the mill mason.

People have I think largely become indifferent to the true significance of those textile mills which are now beginning to look so picturesque in their settings of woodland, moor and stream. For their first quarter of a century, and longer – that is until mechanical looms came into general use – they were all spinning mills which were operated by women and children. It is as such that you must imagine those little Hells, those innumerable, profit-making little Belsens in their idyllic settings of woods and streams. In their present ruin, they are becoming 'picturesque' for the second time round. One image that sticks in my mind and will not go away is of the coach parties of ladies and gentlemen, in their silks and top hats perhaps, who used to complete their tours of more usual romantic sights of the north – of waterfalls, of Gordale Scar, of the spectacular limestone dales further north – with a *frisson* before the fiery furnaces and clankings of a spinning mill.

And today, after a glimpse of what that tombstone suggested, even the stream which made these prisons and torture-chambers possible seemed, like those visitors in search of the picturesque, to be mocking its victims by virtue of its ignorant laughter; indulging its pearly beauty, shining over waterfalls, and running a deep, rich brown colour in its pools.

It was all these tiny laughing streams, the water that pours everywhere in West

Yorkshire, that did it; that made it all possible. The tiny rills described by Defoe in the eighteenth century forcing their way between stones and grass, spilling through walls, worming from trough to trough and making such marvellous music, especially noticeable on a quiet night, are still there. On this day along the Dean the water-ouzels were singing from the stones.

Before it drove the mills and washed their cloth, before it was carefully treasured in so many 'lodges', dykes, and 'goyts' (water courses), the water was worshipped in a different fashion. Below the graveyard where the orphans are buried is Jerusalem Farm. It is still a traditional picnic ground, and in the nineteenth century one of those places (like the Hardcastle-Crag woods in Hebden Bridge) to which parties of holiday-making mill-workers would go. The sulphur-springs near Jerusalem Farm were supposedly curative; at a deeper level of significance they were magical and the focus for May Day ceremonies.

A beggar named John Preston, of whom it was said that he never slept in a bed, save during one spell in a workhouse, used to preach a 'sermon' here every May Day. Work-people walked to the spa-spring from miles away and the height of the holiday was to persuade the (believe it or not) reputedly shy Preston to perform his 'service'. It was a proper religious job, with hymns, (favourites being 'Rock of Ages' and 'Jesus, Lover of my Soul'), a half-hour discourse on the goodness of the Creator as illustrated by the appearance of the Dean that day, whether there was rain, shine, or even snow, and then, of course, an 'offering', sometimes as much as a pound sterling, which the preacher later spent in the 'Cat'i'th'Well' public house. The beggar's services at the spring were so popular that the minister of the Congregational Chapel took them over, and the Salvation Army came to rival Preston also.

There are other signs and symptoms of the magic and mystery of springs in the Calder Valley area. It is said that beginning on Spa Sunday (the May-Day festival) in 1890, a patch of whitewash mysteriously appeared on a stone above the spring near North Dean Chapel at Luddenden every year before the festival, and no one discovered who so regularly placed it there. At the sulphur spring at Simm Carr, Shibden, the Halifax Temperance Society used to gather on Spa Sunday to preach the virtues of drinking water; following them, the Labour Party remembered the first Sunday in May by meeting here.

Finally, whilst on the subject of water, we might recall the temperance-philanthropist at the village of Norland, above Sowerby Bridge, who converted the cellars of his house into a reservoir. An immense structure it is, for the mere drinking fountain that it appears to be, according to the plaque on the wall:

PRO BONO PUBLICO
Here's that which is too weak to be a sinner.
HONEST WATER
That ne'er let man in'th'mire.

A Methodist graveyard above Jerusalem Farm, Luddenden: the grave of orphans employed in a factory.

Too large unless you believe the cynical version: that he built it in order to sell the water to the mills in the valley, who sooner or later during a dry spell were going to need it – as he had first draw of the water from the hillside, and moreover was holding it back!

Norland is in the direction in which I travelled. Norland Moor, with its 'rocking stone' balanced on the level edge of the plateau, appears to block the end of the Calder Valley. I was retracing approximately the route which I had followed by van a few days previously, but now instead of following the main road I went through the lanes over the hillside. There are innumerable, easily forgotten, ways to follow, all of them tortuous passageways up or down amongst the stones; beyond the falling walls are enclosures of neglected grass, fringed with heather and whinberry. But from this eastern side of the Calder Valley, looking across towards Sowerby, you can see, marvellously preserved, as typical a traditional weavers' landscape as you might find anywhere. Sloping down from the Georgian tower of Sowerby are still those precious little walled enclosures of the hand-loom weavers, where through generations of labour they have shifted and broken the scattered stones and boulders, built walls, planted and manured grass, always struggling to keep at bay the encroachments of the moor so that they might have somewhere to grow oats, keep poultry, and stretch their cloth as it used to be done, on tenter frames in the open air.

In our present age, when we are preserving so many *buildings*, surely an expanse of landscape such as this one deserves saving in total; a shed put up by a farmer, a wall cleared to make space for a tractor, or a line of telegraph poles could ruin it. I fear for it especially because most people, I have observed, pay little attention to this landscape on the edge of Halifax above the industrial mess of the lower part of the Calder Valley, which could if they considered it for a while bring them some delight and interest; enough, at least, to while away a 'boring' journey.

Halifax begins with a collection of houses at King Cross, Friendly, and Pye Nest. Here Adelaide Shaw lived, in comfortable welfare-state retirement, thank goodness. She was seventy-nine, but her face since the time of her photograph had aged so little that her cheeks could still have been those of a fifteen-year-old girl. As I spoke to her, she was repeatedly anxious lest her story was of no interest to anyone, particularly 'the young'.

'I was born at a farm up Soyland. My father had a lot of bad luck. He wasn't farming then, he was a paper finisher – they used to count the reels as they came from the mill. He kept going to a job and then something happened so he went to another one and we were moved around quite a bit. In those days a lot of mills were burnt down. That at Ripponden was burnt. When a mill burnt down they couldn't stand around in the

Halifax.
'My heavens are brass, my earth is iron, my moon a clod of clay,
My sun a pestilence burning at noon, and a vapour of death in the night.'

village, they had to walk somewhere and get something else. It happened quite a few times and I suppose he got a bit frustrated and he went to America when I was about thirteen. He worked his passage across and only stayed about twelve months. My father farmed from then on, except when he took it into his head he would go and have a fish shop in Halifax up Hanson Lane. It did well, but we used to be open until twelve o'clock at night and standing over this fish shop wouldn't do for my mother who'd always been in the fresh air in the country. My father used to take her for a walk up Hanson Lane every night after twelve o'clock. "Well, this won't do at all,' he says. "I'll go back to farming."

'We started farming again when I was seventeen. We lived at The Breck, and at Red Brink on Crow Hill. Red Brink belonged to the chapel, I don't know whether it had been left to them or something. Most of my mill life was spent up the hillside there. He farmed up at Kebroyd. Then when my mother died we came to live in Halifax and so my husband and I persuaded him to live at a cottage up the roadside there. But he always wanted farming and he used to look at his hands and say, "Look at these hands." We'd answer, "What's the matter with them?" "Oh, I'd rather have a spade in my hands than a fork." He didn't like retiring. He used to go often to look at the farm when it was rented out, just to do bits. They only have horses there now. My father would turn in his grave if he knew it was trampled up with riding horses – because he was a dairy farmer, and that was that.

'We used to pay threepence or fourpence a week to go to school. When we left we got so many marks from the teacher to say whether we were fit and intelligent enough to go to work. The men that were the overlookers used to be looking out for girls that were leaving school and two or three asked my mother if I could go and work in their mill. My sister started when she was twelve. I wasn't very strong: I don't know why I had to go in to the mill because every now and then I had to have nearly a month off poorly. My dad realised I wasn't very strong but I don't think it was ever thought you could do anything else. They were poor and they needed the money and as soon as they had a worker that was it, you had to work to bring some money home and so you didn't care about your health. All our parents ever thought about was work, work. I don't think most people ever left the village, you know. If my mother went to Halifax she used to reckon she was going a long way. She used to bring us a present back of a penny bar – they were squares of chocolate. But when he went to America my father did say I wasn't to go in the carding room at the mill on no account. He said I could go anywhere else but not in the carding, and it did cause a bit of trouble with my uncle, and I went doubling. That was hot in the doubling but it wasn't dirt. Carding made that fluff – it's scrubbing the cotton off. It was a bit like that candy floss that you buy. But I think it was being confined in the mill for so long that in the end – I was twenty-five when I gave up – my father said: "Well, it seems you're not going to keep up. It's going to keep getting at you, is the mill." Funnily enough after that I've been stronger than my sister.

Wainhouse Tower, Halifax: a folly in the style of a chimney – 'The Athens of the Industrial Revolution'.

Adelaide Shaw (extreme right) in 1913. 'It's a different age now. I wouldn't say anything wrong about it but I think we enjoyed our young days just as much in another way.'

'It was all new machinery when I went to the mill. It was lovely. Everything shone, you had to clean it and clean it with white linen. All the beginners were doffers – they were mugs, like, running around fetching the bobbins. We used to fill this big basket on wheels, that we called a "skip", with bobbins and wheel it up to these long machines and put the bobbins on. We were too small to reach the machinery so we used to get a piece of wood that we called a "broych" that had the cops on so we could reach with the bobbins. The machines were what they called "ginnies". They used to come together – like that. The space between they called the "ginny gate". You could get through this little bit when the ginnies were out but if they were coming together you'd to make a dash for it to get out of the way.

'We started at six o'clock. We had to be up before six and we worked until half-past five at night and I lived right on the hilltops. We had to work all the time, there was no breaks. We didn't have a cup of tea in the middle of the morning or anything like that.

'The bosses used to walk up and down. We hadn't to sit down, you know. I don't know what they'd think if they had to go back to what we did. There was nowhere to make a cup of tea if you wanted one. We used to take our food packed up. There was nowhere to warm anything. We used to go to the engineer's home and she had a boiler with a tap on it where we used to queue up with our pots, tea and sugar or cocoa or whatever we were having. There she was, stood at a table with a milk jug and a spoon; and we paid threepence a week for that.

'You daresn't be late back. The overlooker used to come into the millyard. The first time you were late he'd just go like that! – and look at his watch. He wouldn't speak but it was as bad as nearly saying something to you. We used to creep past him and go in. But if you were late two days together he'd give you a good swearing at and say, "See this doesn't happen agin." But if it did happen, I've known him send them back – and you had to come again at half-past eight. And you'd gone there for six o'clock. He was very strict, but he got the work out of them.

'I remember one winter it was snowed up so much that the lane was level. The lane was cut out of the fields, and the fields on top and the lane was filled up with snow and we couldn't get out. It had to be dug out before we could go to work. My brother worked at Thorpe Mill – is it a mill now, Thorpe Mill? – and it was breakfast time before we could get to go to work. There's a lot of broken cars there now, isn't there? He got there at breakfast time and they sent him right back. Right up to the top there! So my father says, "Right," he says, "you're not going back." "Oh!" he says, "I'll have to go back, I'll have to." "No," my father says, "you're not going back. Come along a me." He went to Sowerby Bridge and got him in at another mill. Then he went to see them at Thorpe Mill and he says, "You want to see what this boy went through to get here." There was no snow in Triangle but it had drifted on the hilltops. My brother stayed on at this second mill until he went driving buses. They all came out of the mill when they could. But there's still good money to be made there now, isn't there?

'There wasn't unions in those days . . . until I got older and then they started. Those that were in the union started coming round and asking us and we had to join. Dugdales always did very fair to us. When we did anything wrong we used to choose four to go to the manager in the office. "Who's going to go?" Well, it was a case of "Will you go, and then I'll go; and I'll go if you'll go with me." We talked to him and he would come out and look at us and at the work and we often got satisfaction. We never used to have trouble but if we had bad work we had to see to it that it was put right.

'Dugdales used to give us a treat once a year. Once it was a double wage and I remember mine was eight-and-six, for Christmas. Another year they gave us a charabanc outing to Morecambe. The charabanc didn't come and collect us like they would now. We'd to go to the top of Luddenden Lane. It was a pouring wet morning and they put this hood up. There was nothing at the side and we were all huddled to the middle because the rain was blowing in, but oh! we thought we had a marvellous time when we went to Morecambe for the day. And then another time they gave us a social and dance. We thought that was nice.

'It was a long walk back home from half-past five. We were too tired to think about going anywhere else. Mother always had a good dinner for us. We were dirty and wanted a wash – there was nowhere to wash at the mill. And we had to put our food up for the next day. "Jock", we used to call it – "putting your jock up". We had a little tin that was divided in the middle, one portion for breakfast, one for tea and sugar, and one for dinner.

'My mother wasn't a very strong woman and we tried to help her at nights. We did a lot of the housework. Monday night we had to finish washing socks and dusters and emptying tubs. The men wore white velvet corded trousers and they were scrubbed every week. I remember my mother scrubbing all the clothes on the table. You had two oak tubs, and a peggy-stick with a lot of legs round the bottom. We used to put the clothes through both of these tubs, back again into the boiler, back again into some clean water, and when you'd got them dry, turn them through the mangle again. They were all nicely folded *before* you ironed them. It must have been hard work for them, mustn't it? On the Tuesday when we got home we used to do the ironing. On the Wednesday she'd be baking all day. The baking bowl and all the dirty utensils were there waiting to be washed. Thursday we had a fireside full of brasses. It used to take me and my sister an hour to clean them all. The fender had a right big knob in the centre where the rods joined, and we got to arguing so much about who should clean this knob that we used to do half each. Then my mother would put an old shawl on the sofa and wrap them all up until Sunday. On Friday we'd to clean all the windows, mop the flags and clean the toilet. At harvest time we'd to get our tea and then go working in the fields until it was dark. When the first world war started, me and my sister had to go round with the milk at weekends, standing on the back of a milk float, not covered up.

I don't think we thought of it as hard work. A lot of people think, oh you were slaves in those days. But we didn't think we were slaves. It was our life and we just did it. On

Saturdays, we worked until dinner time. It'd be half-past one when we got home. We were so glad sometimes to be at home and not go into the bottom again. Sometimes at the Sunday School we used to have a social evening and that wasn't very far. Sunday was started off with Sunday School at nine o'clock; then back home, change your dress, and go to church. But we didn't go out through the week – we were too tired, you know, and then we lived too far away up on the hilltops and we didn't want to come down to Sowerby Bridge. We only went to things that were at the chapel.

'It was the only time we could get dressed up, was Sunday – only time we got without our clogs. But we only had one Sunday dress. Your second best would be the one that had been Sunday's two years before. If you got a nice coat for winter it had to do two years at least; and the same for a summer coat. You wore up your old clothes in the mill, and the same for shoes. You only had two pairs of shoes. I've more pairs of shoes now than I've ever had in my life. I always wore clogs in the mill but I used to put boots on to come home. They used to button up the sides nearly to the knee, and you always carried a button hook with you. I remember having a pair with twenty-four buttons. We got up half asleep to go to the mill at half-past five in the morning and I used to fasten every other button because I hadn't time for them all. But it would be dark and I used to run down that drive to the mill with my every other button loose.

'If ever we went out we had to be in by nine o'clock at night. And it *had* to be nine. It hadn't to be five past. Father always knew where we'd been. We couldn't just say we were going out. It was a case of, we didn't go out if we hadn't somewhere to go, so we'd have to tell a white lie probably if we were off somewhere we shouldn't. In war time they gave dances to gain money to send parcels to the soldiers and of course we were allowed to go to them because it was for a good cause. And we would see boys there; but even then you wouldn't be about with them. You'd be at one side and the boys would be over there – but of course if they wanted you to dance they had to come and ask you. But we didn't mix a lot with them.

'In those days things were rather too much one way and now they're too much the other. I don't think they're getting as much out of life as they could do. It's all for themselves now. I think they miss the real values when they live just for themselves. I know now, living by myself, my life was happier at home. I remember we used to go running up that lane to Red Brink and my brother used to run faster and say, "*Come on! Put your skates on, it's getting five minutes to nine!*" and I'd answer, "Well I can't run any faster, you get in first and it'll be all right!" My dad used to look at the clock if it was turning nine.

'I remember the first time I went out with my husband. I was nineteen and it was the Zion Chapel anniversary. It was a great do then. Zion used to be so full that they put seats out on the front for people that couldn't get in and seats all up the sides of the corridors. I used to go to my mother-in-law's for tea – I was friends with his sister, not with him then – and he brought me home that night. He said, "We won't go Triangle way" (you know, down the road) "we'll make our way over the hill." When we got on the hilltop I said, "Shall we get there for nine o'clock?" and we ran all over those hills to get back for nine.

'I remember my sister when she was courting. I had scarlet fever at the time. In those days if you were out of the Borough they wouldn't take you away; but you'd to be isolated, so they took everything out of one bedroom, so it was just bare boards and my bed and a chair for my mother and a little table. I had to stay there for about eight weeks. I was thirteen weeks off work with this scarlet fever. She used to go out in the yard, did my sister, and look up at the window and tell me all her tales of woe. She was in tears one day. "I was late home last night and it was only ten past but my father *has* given it to me! I wouldn't care," she says, "I wouldn't care if he'd finished one night, but he started again the night after!"

'You know where the Long Chimney is? There used to be a big house there. Is it still standing? We used to ride on the top of the tram so we could look over the big garden. There were some people there called McDougal-Rawsons and every Sunday morning they used to come up in a coach and pair, he in his grey silk top hat and her in all her finery. She was a very fine woman and we used to think it was marvellous because she had such beautiful things and they were nice people. We used to go to the gate about ten o'clock and we used to say, "We'll see if we can catch the McDougal-Rawsons coming up," and they used to come up in style and they always waved to us. Like royalty. They used to go up there to church and we used to think it was marvellous.

'At Whitsuntide we all walked in the Processions. There was no such thing as not walking at Whitsuntide – the little ones first and then the big ones. We used to go to Jerusalem Farm on picnics. There was a place up Bogden called Little London. And there was a little place called New Zealand. We'd set off over the hills and we'd maybe have a shilling or two shillings, that's about all – that was when we were older. When we were younger our mothers would always give us the same as the other girls, sixpence or threepence or whatever it was. If my mother gave us threepence we had to bring some of it back; but she didn't give us less money, because she didn't want us to look so poor that we hadn't anything.

'It's a different age now. I wouldn't say anything wrong about it but I think we enjoyed our young days just as much in another way. We perhaps missed out on a lot of things but on the other hand we were kept together a lot more than they are today. We saw each other every day for years and years and at Sundays we'd see some different ones. We'd our Sunday School and we'd our pals there and we'd go for a walk on Sunday afternoons, so I don't think they get much more now.

'We don't say these things because we're frightened that people have got an image of old people going on about the past and they think it's a bore. That's why we don't say anything. But we have a laugh when we get together, any of us, about things we used to do. When we get together we have a real laugh and a real natter: but we don't when there are any young people because we think they're not interested.'

Holdsworth's Mill, Halifax.

Apart from the impact of noise, it is the quality of light that has always struck me upon entering a mill. In quiet corners amongst the newly-arrived coils of wool, called 'tops', and on the stone stairways, the sunlight lingers in dusty shafts, whilst in other places it is sedately reflected from oiled metals; this is the peaceful, sacramental light of caves, castles and cathedrals. In the spinning and weaving sheds, on the other hand, machines, so rapid that the eye cannot catch them, scatter the brilliant fluorescent light. Here and there it picks out the coloured spots of a weaver's scarf or overall amongst the silver of metal and bits of flying wool. The light throbs, flickers, melts, and changes like the heart of a sunrise.

The tops are like large, white, soft cushions of wool unwinding gracefully all through the working day into the machines. Then the noisy hammering begins as the tops are drawn into fine fibres, and then twisted together, back to their original thickness, but stronger. In their flight through the mill the threads spread out in a huge fan of light. Drawing, finishing, spinning, soft-winding, dyeing, twisting and steaming, to make it ready for weaving; then warping, weaving, winding, inspection and mending, before it goes to the finishers. So, in room after room, the yarn travels as threads of light through the machinery and its heavy thundering.

The weaver is an aristocrat, and she works the harder for the sake of her status. She could instead, for instance, work at 'mending'. Then she would sit in a quiet, clean room, enjoy leisurely chats with her friends, listen to Radio 1, and not be rushed by remorseless machinery, whilst she checks over the pieces that come from the looms. But a conviction that she is practising a superior skill makes a girl become a weaver. To watch her is to see someone apparently conjuring with light itself. As they are spun off the bobbins, the threads convulse like electric sparks in the brilliant light. It's magic to see a spinner or a weaver joining together two of these writhing threads of light.

To watch Shirley, for instance, who is a 'cap-spinner' at Leigh Mills, Pudsey. She is a woman near to retirement, employing an outdated and difficult method. Soon her machine is to be scrapped and not replaced. She has been a cap-spinner in the one mill for twenty-seven years, and doesn't want to change. Her working clothes are carpet slippers and a floral overall; and her way with these vast, noisy, high, banging machines (tending several of them at a time), is as natural and homely as if she were going about domestic tasks in her own kitchen.

Working with several hundred others in the factory, yet Shirley is alone, isolated by the noise. Spinners and weavers converse through lip-reading. In a northern town you will see textile workers (or rather, you used to see them) mouthing silent conversations at one another across busy streets.

I was staring awestruck at her sleight-of-hand with the writhing threads, and she laughed. She spoke to me, assuming that I could lip-read. When I couldn't understand her, she came close, dusting the machines with a bundle of feathers as she approached. She shouted in my ear. She wanted to know what I was doing, and I told her that I was writing a book.

'I gave 4,000 books to the hospital!' she shouted. 'My walls were damp so I had them all in polythene bags behind a curtain in the bedroom. There's not much point in that, is there?'

A bobbin on her spinning-frame ran out of thread. She returned to it, replaced the bobbin, and knotted the ends of the threads. I tried to catch her motions but saw no more than a changing flicker in a streak of light.

She came back to shout in my ear again. 'I'd rather read than watch television,' she said. 'People watch television and they want everything they see and it gives them ideas about violence and sex. People are too selfish these days, it's "dog eats dog" all the time. They're never satisfied.

'Women I know here, when they get to my age, complain that their husbands aren't as fit as they used to be and can't do as much for them, but with me and my husband there's still friendship after sex has finished.

'This country'll never come to anything,' she concluded, 'until the women say to their husbands, "Go out and do some work, or there's no dinner nor nothing else."'

When I left the mill, rooks were nesting in the trees in the rambling garden of what had once been the mill-owner's house, the birds' cries to my deafened ears seeming faint, so faint . . .

8

From Pye Nest I walked steeply downhill to Sowerby Bridge. Few towns could be as splendidly sighted and conceived, as well as so unappreciated, and as neglectfully wrecked, as Sowerby Bridge. It has a wonderful position amongst the hills, at the confluence of two rivers, the Calder and the Ryburn. A higher-than-eye-level look at the main street will show what a splendid town it has been. At eye-level there appear ordinary shop-fronts, but look above and see what splendid Victorian and Edwardian architecture is still left from the original buildings. The centre of the main street is now scarred by a burnt mill, which caught fire shortly after moves were made to preserve it because of its historical interest and its architectural quality; it was one of the earliest brick mill buildings, eighteenth century, with a courtyard that might have been a place of great beauty. On the opposite side of the road is a recently built supermarket, which an aesthetically-minded council might have required to be erected within the walls of what is now a destroyed mill, thus making use of what was considered to be a 'white elephant'. Even before this date, Sowerby Bridge demolished many of its fine and worthy houses, and built incongruous blocks of flats. The splendid railway station (associated with Branwell Brontë), like the above-mentioned mill, caught fire at the time when no one knew quite what to do with it. A town wrecked almost beyond recovery is not unusual in West Yorkshire, though.

There are lots of things I do appreciate about Sowerby Bridge – such as what remains of the close conjunction of mill and town, including the surviving pie-shops and the little cafés selling early morning breakfasts, originally for mill-workers; and the good humour which is usually found amongst those who dwell and work together – people are isolated when they have no common and traditional economy intermingling with their domestic lives, as in the suburbs. A minor, but still very real joy to me in the Halifax district are those most professional stores where you can buy all the tools and parts you might need for any practical job under the sun. The reason they exist is, again, because of the textile mills. They were originally mill-wrights and mill furnishers. After the demise of the factories they still, apparently, scorn to become trivial and tawdry 'D.I.Y.' shops. Somebody, somewhere, in some book or memorial, has to remember those patient people at Sutcliffe's, Bancroft's, and elsewhere, who have so many times given thoughtful and craftsmanlike attention to my problems of whether to use a no. 8 or no. 10 gauge screw, and who have searched so diligently on my behalf through their stores. I have lived in other parts of England, and never found such places. There is a kind of poetry about such care and completeness, and in its way it reflects something about the region.

Half a mile beyond Sowerby Bridge, on the Ripponden road, I cut off to the left through the woods, passed one of the mills derelict along the river course, and went uphill steeply to Norland Moor. This is a surviving piece of common land, unenclosed, and amongst its heather you get a real sense of pre-industrial England.

At the side of the Greetland–Barkisland road on the far side of Norland Moor is Mr Nicholls' mill. You can see little more of it than the roof, because the yard is filled with stacks of tables, chairs, benches, filing-cabinets, metal baskets and timber from demolished mills and houses.

Inside, down narrow passages between the packed banks of old leather, fifteen feet high and thirty feet deep, Mr Nicholls and his assistant Mr Moore were moving a heavy bench of unplaned timbers that was stained with spilled oil. They had unloaded it off a cart, edged it between the warped and rain-bleached chairs, the rusting filing-cabinets and burst baskets, to the door. Here a blackbird had made her nest on top of the stacked timbers and Mr Moore had positioned a sheet of plywood to protect her and her nestlings; she sat tight, tense and bold, and I could see her yellow beak pointing bright as a gun out of the blackness of her body and of her nest.

Mr Nicholls and Mr Moore paused to calculate. They were going to fit this bench in between a hanging cluster of iron paraffin flares (that were as bright a yellow as the blackbird's beak) and a dozen baths and sink-tops.

'I think those bolt holes situated in a four-be-four piece signify its use as some type of a base for a machine lathe, Mr Nicholls,' remarked Mr. Moore.

Thus they address one another, although they have worked together for decades.

'I think you'll find it's held a tank for paraffin or maybe diesel oil somewhere, Mr Moore,' Mr Nicholls quietly corrected him. 'Good morning, Mr Hughes. Are you looking for anything in any special line? Or just looking around?'

Mr Nicholls secured his end of the bench in order to fish around for his packet of Capstan double-strength cigarettes. His skin is grey and he is a compulsive smoker.

'I'd just like to have a look round, Mr Nicholls. To see what's new.'

'Yes, thank you, very good.'

I am aware that to be allowed to *look around* is a privilege, for this mill is broken into on average once a year. 'Usually proper methodical industrial burglars,' Mr Nicholls says. Many of them, he thinks, are scrap-dealers, who call upon him six times a year, not to buy anything, but to see what he has and where he keeps it, so that they know where to look when they return, in the night, with a lorry. Recently too Mr Nicholls has suffered from a pyromaniac. A local boy came by, with a carrier-bag full of wood shavings and a bottle of paraffin, and later sat on the hill-side to enjoy the sight of burning hen sheds, carpenters' shops and mill yards.

'A very useful bench for someone with a greenhouse,' Mr Nicholls remarked. 'Put plants on it. Very unusual to have a bench as long as this.'

'I don't have a greenhouse. I was wondering if you had any of those doors left.'

'Thank you,' answered Mr Nicholls. 'I'll tell you what size they are in a moment. Yes, thank you.'

He opened his spectacles case and took from it a piece of a cigarette packet. He has little notes to himself everywhere. Telephone numbers are written on scraps of timber which, in consequence, may not be moved. Pinned to the doors are cryptic notes hoarded as obsessively as the stacks of rotting leather, with their sickening smell that blows hotly out of the building when you open the door. For Mr Nicholls is really a great collector, and because of this it is impossible to bargain with him – he would just as soon keep his goods. His wife 'puts it all down to his mother', who was a 'hoarder', 'saving bits of string and jam jars'. In the same fashion, her son has caches of Capstan double-strength, which might never be smoked or even discovered again, hidden all over the house. One packet hidden in his best suit, one under linen in a drawer . . .

'They're a standard fitting for a door, six foot two by three foot six.' Then he corrected himself: 'Just a bit bigger than standard.'

It didn't really matter; how could I carry doors with me, anyway? All I wanted was an excuse for calling. 'I'll just have a look around,' I said.

'Yes. Thank you, Mr Hughes.'

When he left school Mr Nicholls was apprenticed to a cabinetmaker. ('I thought I'd be a furniture king.') But he contracted meningitis. The doctor blamed it on the dust from the sandpaper and the wood, but Mr Nicholls thinks 'it was some germ I picked up from the sea on a holiday to Southsea when I was twenty-one.' He seemed to believe that it was the just reward of those who stray out of Yorkshire. He sold vacuum cleaners for a year. Then he entered his uncle's Dickensian office amongst the cloth-traders in the Halifax Piece Hall. They collected off-cuts of leather from local tanneries, graded them into different qualities, thicknesses, lengths and 'square-size measure' and sold them, mostly for saddlery, but also on a stall at Huddersfield Market. ('This was what was known as the waste leather trade.')

Eventually Mr Nicholls had this, his own little mill building, which he converted into a tannery and where he made belting for machinery in Lancashire cotton mills.

Until then Mr Nicholls was adaptable to the times, buying, selling, and manufacturing. He began to lose his trade when the mills changed to using bonded rubber-and-canvas belting instead of leather. He lost it entirely in the 1950s, when the cotton mills themselves went out of business, the government hastening the process by subsidising the scrapping of machinery.

The neighbours, on what during the 1930s had become a genteel suburban road, began to write letters to the local paper and to the clerk of the Council, complaining of the unsightliness of the mill which Mr Nicholls was stocking with his purchases from Lancashire mill-auctions. Engineering equipment, weft and yarn boxes, baskets and skips, office and canteen equipment; and also the household stuff that tended to end up in the attics of mills in the days when the owner lived next to his factory – furniture, Victorian and Edwardian clothes, books and out-of-date pictures.

'What's he doing with that unsightly rubbish over there?' the neighbours asked Mrs Nicholls. 'When's he going to stop?'

They might well ask. In those days there were two mill-closures per week. Mr Nicholls reckons that he visited about 600 auctions. He had found his vocation.

This is one of the parts of England where the population diminished between the 1851 census and 1960. As the Calder Valley prospered so much in the 1850s, and the little farmsteads on the hilltops flourished, providing the towns in the valley with food, and the cotton and worsted mills along the streams with children as labourers, so its collapse from that date onwards is more dramatic, its decline more sordid. Until the last ten years there were ghost villages, like Mill Bank, Heptonstall or Wycoller. (The last until recently was a totally deserted hamlet, gathered around the windowless stone shell of Wycoller Hall, the original Ferndean Manor of Charlotte Brontë's Jane Eyre.)

Industrial society broke down into huge dumps in abandoned quarries or old mill buildings like that of Mr Nicholls. The traditional acceptance of untidy surroundings ('where there's muck there's brass') makes untidiness easier. Abandoned furniture, mattresses and sofas, are a common sight at the sides of moorland roads. Jimmy Nicholls' mill, swamped in demolition-timber and scrap like something that a tidal wave has swept up out of the towns, is as characteristic of contemporary millstone-grit country as any other feature.

Around me, when I left, was the Yorkshire night; one not scented with blossoms, or damp earth, or centuries of manure, as in other rural places, but rich in its own special sounds. At the head of this valley, whilst I was looking for somewhere to stay for the night, perhaps a moorland pub high above the housing estates, I could hear the factories. Their incessant knockings, steady as the dripping of a tap, and broken by outbursts – a jet of steam, or steel sheets thundering onto a floor – played against the murmur of the wind or against the breeze rattling through dry grass stalks. There was a curlew's cry (repeated cuts of sound, sharp as a razor) and the music of streams. Before one faded behind me, another was growing louder as I approached, harmonising with it. I travelled through a rising and falling scale of delicate music that reached out of the moors which were no more than huge black walls, their curved tops floating under a gentle grey sky where a few stars darted out for seconds and then were doused under the flying clouds. On the horizon in one direction the night sky was coloured by a lurid orange spread from street lamps onto the undersides of clouds, whilst in the other direction, from the foot of the valley, a dark mass of fog was approaching, a sticky fluid that made me want to stay on the hill tops.

I remembered how once, after staying for a few months in a city, I went to Heptonstall at night and was thrilled to feel in the darkness about me these vast, imponderable valleys, sanded with golden lights; sensing, even through hearing alone, the life of the moors in the dark – a restless curlew; the scream when two shrews met in the grass; the far barking of a dog, its harshness mellowed by distance; geese; the clank of buckets; a distant factory pulsing; or the streams.

It wasn't easy to find somewhere to stay, not easy at all. Keeping between moor and town I struggled along the lacings of narrow roads. Few people lived here, yet all the roads had street-lighting; a characteristic that gives this part of Yorkshire at night the look of a crowded city. I ascended and descended 'snickets' – footpaths, usually cobbled or paved, often lit just like the roads, and walled often on both sides. Some paths go for miles through fields, woods and moor, seeming today to have little purpose to them. In other counties they are old, pre-industrial routes, spread out like wheel-spokes from the parish church. Here in West Yorkshire the centre of the pathways is more often a mill, and they were for the workers travelling from moorland hamlets. The paths were built as thoroughly as the mills; lots of them were made in the 1830s by out-of-work weavers employed by the parish councils under a system whereby, in order to receive poor-rates, they were forced to work on the roads, and it is largely to this that we owe the engineered footpaths and the well-constructed moorland lanes of West Yorkshire.

Suddenly, rising over the rest of a dark slope, I stumbled onto a pub dramatically over-lit on an empty road. The bright lights in the forecourt threw shadows that made the front of the building like a clown's mask. I went inside. The Snug and the Tap Room had been 'knocked through', making a large room that was filled with brothel-like equipment of whips, daggers, manacles, polished chains and harnesses. There was a padded bar and polystyrene, or photographed, wood or stone surfaces; despite this, over the bar a fake-Gothic parchment outlined the history of the building that 'went back to the fourteenth century'.

The landlady, or barmaid, was saying to the one customer already present, 'You ask him. He'll bloody clout me if I do.' Then she calmly described how her husband had once beaten her for wearing curling pins in her hair when she went to bed.

I needn't have bothered thinking about staying here for the night. 'We stopped doing guests, love, it isn't worth it. No, you won't find anywhere nearer than town.' So I went out and stumbled again through the stony fields.

It was hopeless to search up here. But, cruising over the moortops, up and down lanes where some would hesitate to drive a Land Rover, was a double-decker bus. So I caught it.

'Who'd want to stay a night in Huddersfield?' said the first landlady I asked when I reached the town.

People were coming home from work. Amongst them there was a special brightness: the clothes of Pakistanis and Indians. They arrive in Oldham, Halifax,

Huddersfield and Bradford clothed in white or patterned textiles, and most of them are eventually taught by the prolonged winters and the insidious dirt to cover their native brightness with drab English clothes. But some are freshly arrived, or do not change their habits; and Huddersfield has one of the largest Pakistani communities in England. They are a people who are virtually never found visiting, let alone living in, the moorland villages, yet they are crowded into the surrounding towns.

I drifted from pub to pub, each sending me on to the next place. I found myself stumbling in the dark mud, the wet cement and windy, unlit spaces of the new roadworks that ring Huddersfield like a fortification. This was no good to me, and I retreated to the town centre again.

Near its vast railway station I stood, embarrassed in my muddy boots, on the carpet of the grandest hotel in town. Luckless once more I was turned away, and directed for half a mile, beyond the roadworks again, to a place kept by a polite Indian who telephoned more hotels for me, in English as immaculate as his clothes. At last I heard that there was a room to be had in a pub called The Miller's Rest, but I got lost following the Indian's directions.

I asked the way of a man tottering out of a pub.

'Come with me, boss, I'll show you. I'm going there,' he said.

'This area was supposed to be a redevelopment area,' he grumbled. 'It was supposed to be made better. And what have they done? They put swings and roundabouts near where old people are living and of course the teenagers are there until goodness knows what time so there's all sorts of goings-on and these old people have no peace at all. It isn't fair, is it, boss?'

I agreed. I was, after all, dependent on him.

'Things have just got worse and worse. All that money that's been put into it has been wasted because what they've done, they've let the Pakistanis in.'

(Christ! What an awful night this was turning out to be!)

'If you don't know these Pakistanis and how they carry on I'll take you for a trot round here sometime and show you some of these houses and you'll wonder why anyone agrees that these people should be allowed into the country. I bought my house twelve or fourteen years ago and altered it no end of a lot. Now we're pestered wi' them sort. They allow two people to sleep in every room including the bathroom . . . there are twelve to fourteen people in the house next to mine . . . there's a house along there I wouldn't keep nanny goats in. These Pakistanis don't use toilets as we do. It's against their religion to sit on a toilet. They stand on the seat. Or they wrap it up in newspaper. I've worked in these mills and it's amazing what trouble the bosses have with them. An instance of one down Oldham – this was the foreman that were telling me this. He went to look round, and the chap on this loom had made a right mess of it, so he went into the office to tell the manager. The boss said, "It can't be. He's one of the best men we have working for us." He said it must be a mistake, so finally they both went to have a look. Well, when the boss saw the chap that were at the lom, he said "Who are you? What are you doing here?" – he didn't recognise him. "Where's so-and-so?" he asked. "Oh, he sell me the job," this chap says. "He go work somewhere else . . ."'

' . . . You going hiking or some'at?' my companion asked me, as if he had just noticed my rucksack.

'I'm having a few days off,' I answered.

'You go to the swimming baths here,' he said, 'it's like jumping in the bloody Ganges.

'Do you know they don't pay income tax for the first twelve months? If *you* start working here, *you* do – and you're bred and born an Englishman. Now you get married – you're a young Englishman. You find your own home. You furnish it. Out of your own pocket. Now these people – they find a house, they get £100 towards the furniture from the government. In one mill, where they was still on coal for the boilers, the engineers wanted someone to help move a load that had been tipped. But it was against the religion of these Pakistanis to shovel coal. Anyway, they come down from the office. "Are you going to move it?" "No. 'Gainst our religion to shovel coal." "Righto," said the boss. "You can have your cards." That made 'em shift it!

'It isn't a case of your wanting to change their religion, or any other thing for that matter. Only their ways of living.'

At last my companion stopped.

Outside a terraced house.

'Is this The Miller's Rest?' I asked him.

He laughed. 'You know that place where I met you? You was standing right by it then. I just wanted your company for a while.' He opened his door. 'Goodnight, boss.'

I made my own way back to The Miller's Rest. All round me the lengthy ceremonies of drunken parting were being acted out outside pub doors.

'Goodnight! Goodnight! Tarra!'

'Neet, then. Tarra!'

'Goodnight!'

Voices faded out of sound. Vomit was spilled over the steps of The Miller's Rest. Inside, the departed tide of customers had left the floor silted with cigarette butts and spilled beer, and the landlady was emptying the ash-trays into it.

'Were you the one that phoned for a room? I was just going to lock up . . .'

9

The next morning I caught a bus to Elland and walked again past Mr Nicholls' mill. Near Crumlin I returned to the open moor. The last building was a farm ringed by abandoned vehicles, where a dog kennelled in a barrel kept the sheep from straying off the open country and down the road towards town. The moor's blow of silence and cold was like being pole-axed. Hillsides were clawed by shadows and from amongst the clouds strings of light shuttled through the shifting brilliances, the red and gold of whinberry and bracken, and of the white acres of dried, sapless grass-stalks. As the wind stirred their sunlit tops, the pale grass seemed to etherealise into a drifting vapour. But I could do no more than take glances at it under the wind. Some distance away a scrap of polythene glittered. Near the roadside an armchair was rotting into the gold and brown of the bog.

The road was empty. At Buckstones it broke onto the edge of a cliff where great boulders tumbled over a huge scoop of moorland. Below me was one reservoir. Far off – how far? – a glittering bar in what seemed to be sky was another sheet of water that caught the sun on a distant moor, the soft greys of which sank into the haze of the sky. This was Wassenden Moor, with Marsden at the foot of it.

In that town there is a mill which is still partly surrounded by the remains of a stone barricade, with loopholes for cannon, built to defend it against the attacks of the Luddites in 1812. That was the year when two Marsden blacksmiths, Enoch and James Taylor, began making 'cropping frames' for local cloth-finishing shops. The machine consisted merely of a pair of hand-shears clamped to a frame and controlled by a wheel to travel over the length of a piece of cloth, clipping off the wooly 'nap' as it moved. Clumsy and primitive as it was, it could be worked by only one man and would do the work of ten hand-croppers.

In the same year, Napoleon's blockade of foreign ports, the war with the United States, and the bad harvests of 1810 and 1811 had made trade difficult, the cost of living high. The cropping frames could save the cloth manufacturers from bankruptcy and many were determined to use them no matter what the opposition. (There is a mill in Clitheroe, Lancashire, that was built like a medieval fortress with a moat around it filled with water, to defend it from the attacking workers. In 1812, three men and a boy of fourteen were executed at Westhoughton, Lancashire, for burning down a cotton mill. Despite such penalties as this in 1826 a mob destroyed almost every loom in Blackburn, Accrington and Darwen.) William Horsfall of Marsden said that he was going to install cropping frames 'even if I have to ride through blood to my saddle-girths to do it'. His threat was put to the test; the croppers, threatened with unemployment and starvation, determined on smashing the frames.

Luddism began in Nottinghamshire as a response to the introduction of stocking-frames. The movement was named, it was said, after one Nedd Ludd, who has however left no historical trace at all. Considering the part played in those early popular movements by notions of an inherited British 'Constitution', an England of the distant past thought of as being just and free, and by mythical leaders ranging from King Arthur to Robin Hood, it is interesting to speculate whether the origin of Ludd might be the Celtic god, *Ludd, Lugh* or *Lough*, who is remembered in so many place names – Louth, Loughborough, London (perhaps) and Luddenden in the Calder Valley – in the festival of Lammas Day (Lough's Mass) and in many other ubiquitous forms. He was our native Apollo and sun-god.

Following the movement's beginnings in Nottinghamshire, West Yorkshire districts too had their groups of Luddites, each led by a 'general' or 'King Ludd'. The King Ludd of the Colne Valley was George Mellor, a hand-cropper of Longroyd Bridge, near Huddersfield. The Luddites – Mellor and two friends from the same shop, Benjamin Walker and Thomas Smith, William Thorpe from a nearby shop and thirty or forty others – made a vow of fraternity that they called being 'twissed in'; meaning that they were now twisted into one body, as wool fibres are twisted into one thread. They threatened mill-owners who used cropping frames. They waged guerrilla warfare, turning their knowledge of the Marsden moors to their advantage against the strange soldiers who were sent to arrest them. They plotted their campaigns at isolated pubs, and they dispersed across the moors when they heard the jangling harness of the Redcoats' horses. They blackened their faces and raided isolated farmhouses to steal firearms, and they drilled amongst the rocks and heather.

As a result of such determined tactics it required 12,000 troops to suppress Luddism in northern England, which was more than were required to conquer Spain in the Peninsula War. With 'Old Enoch' (the name they gave to a heavy hammer, called after Enoch Taylor so that they could use, as a rallying cry, 'Enoch makes them and Enoch breaks them') the Luddites smashed a load of cropping frames being delivered across Liversedge Moor. They broke into mills at night to smash frames; and during an attack on Rawfold's Mill, Liversedge (which appears in Charlotte Brontë's novel *Shirley*) two Luddites were killed. As a reprisal for this, George Mellor organised the murder of William Horsfall on Crosland Moor, on market day, 28 April 1812. Though most people in the Colne Valley knew who the murderers were the secret was kept, despite a £2,000 reward, until the autumn, when the Luddites were betrayed by one of their own members, Benjamin Walker. After this the movement lost its strength. Other Luddites became 'untwissed', as breaking the oath was called. Trials of the Luddites took place in York in January 1813. Many croppers were transported and the murderers, with the exception of Walker, were hanged – Walker, when released from prison, returned and lived to an old age in the Colne Valley, despised by his neighbours.

Mills in the Colne Valley, Huddersfield. 'Contrast the grandeur of those events of the past and the blight of insignificance that affects our neglected region now.'

You can choose whether to see the Luddites as foolish pursuers of a lost cause, as early Chartists learning how to fight, or even, in their opposition to mills and machinery, as the first environmentalists.

The latter aspect I once expressed in a poem, 'The Luddite Chapel'. Many of the Luddites were Methodists, who had gained their elementary education in Sunday Schools, and after their execution they wished to be buried in Methodist graveyards. This was forbidden by Jabez Bunting, then a local superintendent (the Jabas Branderham of *Wuthering Heights*, '– good God – what a sermon! divided into four hundred and ninety parts . . . '), who later became a national Methodist leader, and a man more influential than any other in making Methodism a Tory and mill-owners' religion. In William Blake's phrase, 'the gates of the chapel were shut/And thou shalt not writ over the door' – to the Luddites the chapel gates were quite literally closed, which led to stormy scenes outside.

When I searched out these sites, there was only quiet dereliction. In a field near one chapel, there was a half-demolished chimney (they were often set many yards from the mill in order to make a long underground flue to cause as strong a draught as possible) set with broken glass, and it was as if revolted, or revolting, Nature herself was striking back with this violent image.

THE LUDDITE CHAPEL

A spot in the sun – a holy site
with battered graveyard front and back
where the Chapel keeps its coke.
Here Jabez Bunting refused
burial to a hanged Luddite,
Saying, 'Methodism hates democracy as much as sin.'

The awesome coughing of its last trustee
hacks amongst the tumbled stones.
She's come to scrub
and tidy flowers into the bin; and would agree
that Adam, expelled from Paradise,
had best get on with his job.

What ruin! A hideous sight –
a chimney demolished to a stump, a dwarfed sheath
set with broken glass like the teeth
of vagina dentata
voracious enough to show their rebellion was right,
breaks into the fields beneath.

The other person I'd like to remember here is the poet Samuel Laycock, born in Marsden in 1826, just after the Luddite and other revolutionary 'disturbances'. Sam, unlike the Luddites, does have a memorial, a rough-cut stone in a Marsden Park.

The poet was not exactly a radical, though he did speak for the feelings of the common man. He experienced hardship from the age of nine when he was working from six in the morning until eight at night in a woollen mill; but most poignantly when his family moved to Stalybridge, in Cheshire, where in the 1860s he suffered the effects of the American Civil War upon the Lancashire cotton trade.

There was, of course, no cotton, no trade, but only complete poverty. An evangelical lady at this time asked a child if she knew the meaning of 'sorrow'. '*Want of cotton,*' the child replied.

Laycock responded by speaking, not down to, but for, his fellow-sufferers. He was able, simply by being one of them, to praise, without it being patronising, the virtues necessary for survival: courage, humour, and family warmth. As a poet he was popular and much read. In 1864 no less than 14,000 people who were near starvation thought it worth a penny or two to buy broadsheets of Laycock's poems. 3,000 copies of the handsome volume of his collected poems, *Warblins Fro' An Oud Songster* (published in Oldham!) were sold. Although he is a fine poet who should be in anthologies of the nation's poetry, today he is so much neglected that I would like to include one of my favourites here: *Welcome, Bonny Brid* ('Bird'). It was written whilst the baby, which it so warily welcomes, was being born – and which Samuel patriarchally assumed would be a boy, though it turned out to be a girl.

WELCOME, BONNY BRID!

Th'art welcome, little bonny brid,
But shouldn't ha' come just when tha did;
    Toimes are bad.
We're short o' pobbies for eawr Joe,
But that, of course, tha didn't know,
    Did ta, lad?

Aw've often yeard mi feyther tell,
'At when aw coom i' th' world misel'
    Trade wur slack;
An' neaw it's hard wark pooin' throo –
But aw munno fear thee, iv aw do
    Tha'll go back.

Cheer up! these toimes'll awter soon;
Aw'm beawn to beigh another spoon –
    One for thee;
An', as tha's sich a pratty face
Aw'll let thee have eawr Charley's place
    On mi knee.

God bless thee, love, aw'm fain tha'rt come,
Just try an' mak' thisel awhoam:
    Here's thi nest;
Tha'rt loike thi mother to a tee,
But tha's thi feyther's nose, aw see,
    Well, aw'm blest!

Come, come tha needn't look so shy,
Aw am no' blamin' thee, not I;
    Settle deawn,
An' tak' this haupney for thisel,
There's lots o' sugar-sticks to sell
    Deawn i' th' teawn.

Aw know when furst aw coom to th' leet,
Aw're fond o' owt' at tasted sweet;
    Tha'll be th' same.
But come, tha's never towd thi dad
What he's to co thee yet, mi lad –
    What's thi name?

hush! hush! tha mustn't cry this way,
But get this sope o' cinder tay
    While it's warm;
Mi mother used to give it me,
When aw wur sich a lad as thee,
    In her arm.

Hush-a-babby, hush-a-bee, –
Oh, what a temper! dear-a-me
    Heaw tha skrikes!
Here's a bit o' sugar, sithee;
Howd thi noise, an' then aw'll gie thee
    Owt tha likes.

We've nobbut getten coarsish fare,
But, eawt o' this tha'll get thi share,
    Never fear.
Aw hope tha'll never want a meal,
But allis fill thi bally weel
    While tha'rt here.

Thi feyther's noan been wed so long,
An' yet tha sees he's middlin' throng
    Wi' yo' o.
Besides thi little brother Ted,
We've one upsteers, asleep i' bed,
    Wi' eawr Joe.

But tho' we've childer two or three,
We'll mak' a bit o' reawm for thee,
    Bless thee, lad!
Tha'rt th' prattiest brid we have i' th'
nest,
So hutch up closer to mi breast;
    Aw'm thi dad.

10

So far I had walked entirely on the eastern side of the Pennines; now I was to make the climb over to the other side. I had to find my way across Standedge; a bleak peat-bog, fifteen hundred feet above sea-level. It is a soggy place like a great sponge, with a railway tunnel underneath it so that stumpy chimneys poke out of the moor, carrying (or which used to carry) smoke from the tunnel.

Up on the hilltop there, as I struggled in and out of peat-gulleys, my face, hands and trousers blackened and wet, I met the spirit of the bog.

Mind you, the peat has more frightening manifestations than the one I met. In certain effects of sunlight and mist huge figures seem to rise up, which are however no more than one's own shadow thrown onto a wall of fog. This spirit was less frightening, but more truly one of Standedge Moor.

He waited at the head of the path and there was no-one but us two upon the whole moor. By his dress and his manner of pacing about as if everything belonged to him he was evidently a farmer. He was unflinchingly studying my approach, even from two hundred yards away projecting something that made me glad that I knew I was on a right of way.

At the very moment when we drew close enough for some greeting to be inevitable, he turned half way round towards the wall, and casually peed. Only us two in the whole world, and that is what he did.

Over the brow of the hill, I fell into Saddleworth with a feeling of gratitude. It must, through the years, have impressed many travellers in the same fashion, to find after fierce boglands the sight of gentler slopes, green, scattered with villages and houses.

Saddleworth is a thin projection of Yorkshire down a long winding valley into Lancashire and Cheshire. Isolated in a foreign county, regarding themselves as Yorkshire villages holding out against the overspilling of industrial Lancashire, it is no wonder that here, especially, they cultivate an identity for themselves. Saddleworth is the general title for a group of villages whose names when pronounced one after another sound like a tune played by a brass band: Dob Cross, Denshaw, Diggle and Delph. This is as it should be, for the bands here, and the annual Festival when the pubs are open all day, are famous. The streets are closed to all but the competing musicians, who must march up and play under the Club window. (This is done so that the judges cannot see them, even though no-one believes that an expert cannot, after half a dozen notes, tell Fodens Motor Works from CWS.)

And here's the place for my favourite brass band story. A victorious band was returning drunk, rejoicing, and still playing its instruments late at night up the main street of its home village. (Whether it was Haworth, Holmfirth, Glossop or Delph I know not, for I have heard this story told of all of them.) Someone out of temper with brass bands leant his, or her, head out of a window and told them to stop making such a row. So the players took off their shoes, or boots, or clogs, and tiptoed over the cobbles – still playing their instruments.

The original 'Saddleworth' – a hamlet built on the hill, at the heart of a widespread desolate moorland parish, when the sites of those other, later villages to which it has given its name were no more than intractable marshes – hardly exists any more. It has been thinned to a scattering of converted cottages. On the site of a succession of churches since Norman times, the existing church is a Victorian building as stark and black as a mill building. If you follow the footpath by the stream down from here, you might stumble through tangled weeds and briars onto the foundations of the original village.

I lived in Saddleworth for eight years, first of all near Delph, then in a cottage named Primrose Cottage, on Primrose Hill. The primroses disappeared long ago and the hill is now covered only by wiry grass which turns, as on every millstone-grit hillside, a most startling, fiery red-gold colour in the autumn rains. Grey sheep wander like the ghosts of lost tribes. The slopes rise to a crest of gritty rocks, sparkling with silica and rain-swept into anthropomorphic shapes, worn into basins which retain water that was once regarded as a magical cure for blindness or diseases of the eyes. Above this is a plateau with in one direction as fierce, or as typical, and deserted a landscape as one could find in the Pennines, where rocky headlands melt or pierce the misty air and there is a sense of immeasurable loneliness. Looking the other way one can see, bright as a needle, the CWS tower-building in the centre of Manchester.

I remember Saddleworth as a place where at certain moments the sombre landscape broke for short periods into vivid life. Spring was always a disappointment; always late, and always brief. But late summer, when the cotton grass bloomed with patches of white in the bogs, was beautiful; and autumn was unique, when mists were tinted purple as they glazed the flowering heather, whilst underfoot and over the banks was a dressing of the brilliant heather flowers, of the yellow of gorse and of the sonorous darkness of the herbage, as well as of that particular fiery colour which I have already mentioned.

It was most exciting when it snowed – the beauty of it, and the vitality it suddenly drew from people! There rarely fell more than a few inches, but our trouble and excitement came when the wind followed and blew perhaps for a week or more. It lifted the snow into the air and kept it boiling in a constant, blinding, maddening fury. The back of our house faced the direction from which the wind whipped off the moors, banking drifts against our wall whilst leaving the high rocks as bare black streaks above the snow fields. The edges of the door, and the window of the lean-to kitchen, we lined with rags and towels which became saturated and froze, for snow fine as salt still drifted through the crannies, whilst the wind outside made it impossible to open up and shovel it away. We used the front door, which was usually more sheltered, for me to fetch coal from the barn. Before I reached the barn, fifteen yards away, it was possible to get lost. I remember often pausing in doubt, icicles forming on my face and beard as I stared, dizzy and drugged by the sight of those frantic patterns in the whirling snow. Day by day we ate our way with increasing fearfulness to the last tins of food. We sat close to the fire, continuously shifting the burned sides of our bodies and warming the sides numbed by the draught, whilst hoping that the snow would not bring down the electricity pylons.

But when the wind at last ceased, a pristine whiteness, as when the cotton grass bloomed, covered the landscape which was given new forms under the drifts. A new muffled quiet came over it. We would see the snow ploughs, the only traffic moving on the hills, their flashing lights reflected on the whiteness day and night.

When the wind stopped blowing it was a signal for everyone to struggle through the drifts by whatever route they could find, down to Uppermill to buy food. All of us at the same moment would go out into this new stillness (having seen nothing of one another for a week) and meet together lower down the road to raid the village in a pack.

In Saddleworth I taught art part-time to some of my neighbours in the local Further Education Institute, and to their children in the local Secondary School; for the first time in my life I gave myself several days a week in which to write poems. I made them out of simple elements, for what else did I have? There were the changes in sky, light and weather over a landscape of rushes, heather and half-secret outbursts of water, with its wandering sheep and its broken farms. There was the industrial and village life of the valleys. So I wrote poems about the smoke rising from the chimney of a distant farm; about the sparse life of farmsteads and hamlets; about the sheep; about the twilights, the snow, and walking on the cold bareness of the moor in winter; and about the few birds that inhabited the moor – the curlews, larks, or flocks of twites and finches. I spent hours of the day or night in walks alone, or in sitting on the cottage step watching the drama of sky and moor.

I had never in my life before spent long periods, day after day through several years and through all the changes of seasons, contemplating the changes over one landscape. From this cottage door, level with the tops of the hills so that they seemed like the crests of waves disappearing northwards towards Northumberland and Scotland, this most solid of landscapes, made of bare rocks and treeless slopes with dark mill towns at their feet, appeared constantly mobile and liquid as it was transformed by the weather. In one valley it might be raining, whilst in another the sun was shining; and I could peer into both of them, watching these islands of weather moving, and guess which was approaching – the clouds often seeming more solid than the hills that they veiled.

I learnt there how varied mists, that constant element in which we lived, could be.

There were mists that seemed as delicate as grey flower petals strewn on the valley floor, and so transparent, their faint edges constantly, subtly changing, that you could tell they were there only in contrast to the rocks and headlands amongst them. There were more solid mists that rocked in the valleys like porridge in a bowl, throwing tongues of vapour into the air and up the sides of the hills. There were fogs that gathered at the valley ends, pushed black fists over the tops of hills, and widened until they engulfed us in a storm of hail or snow.

I watched that countryside almost as much during the night as I did during the day. One summer night, whilst I was concentrating on a poem, I was startled by a noise outside. The most familiar sound can be frightening if you do not expect it, and this one was no more than that of stones falling off a wall; something that happens at the slightest disturbance on these hills laced with old drystone walls. I went to the door. A full moon had risen over an utterly clear landscape, the blue hills running like a frozen sea, and a flock of sheep attracted by my light had gathered around the cottage. As they stood in a semi-circle their eyes shone jade-green in the light. The sheep, like the whole landscape of boulders and hills, were petrified. It made the moment magical, as if it was outside time. Then suddenly the spell was broken. One of the sheep panicked away and the others followed, clattering up the hillside.

The magic was in the ordinary having turned into the unexpected, and that night, abandoning the poem over which I had been labouring for hours, I quickly wrote a better one, 'Beasts':

At night, surrounding the house,
their fear impregnates summer air
as muffled and crazy as moths
they stumble amongst the gorse.

What's that? What's that?
Laying poems aside, I go to see.
They stare: as if my stare
stunned them. Then race,

fleece combed in gorse and wire
towards a moorline stark as cold black iron
in the twilit midnight, under the moon . . .

My landlord, who was also my only neighbour for some distance, must have thought, as he saw me sitting on the steps of my cottage, that I spent most of my time taking breaks from writing. Sometimes he seemed offended and irritated by this, because he had to go to work. But he himself also was, as they say, a little bit 'yonderly' – meaning for ever looking yonder, that is into the distance, dreamily, so that he stumbled over what was immediately present. He was an amateur artist. Like nearly all the members of the local art group he used to paint hill landscapes in the drab, military grey style of L. S. Lowry. Only he, underneath, was more flamboyant and I suspected he'd like to do as Gauguin did, throw off his job as a clerk, and even if he was too timid to go off to the tropics, perhaps to stay at home, live off whatever came his way, as I did, and paint hill landscapes. Smoking his pipe he liked to come and tell me art-group gossip, who had been there to 'give us a talk' and so on, and resentfully to praise my everlasting, ever-surprising good fortune (as it seemed to him). 'If you fell off the Co-op cart you'd land in the dividend,' he said.

But he spent most of his spare time labouring to make out of a stony slope a lawn and a garden – of a kind that gardeners in level countryside often painfully imitate with rockeries and with plants such as heather that are difficult to grow in fertile places but which are natural to Primrose Hill. My neighbour, on the other hand, struggled to level out the hillside and to stock it with the flowers that could barely survive on an exposed and rocky place; what snow, frost, or wind did not destroy, the sheep did, determinedly breaking or jumping walls and fences because of the lack of succulent food outside the garden. I learnt that there were hardly any plants other than foxgloves that these sheep, at any rate, couldn't eat; which was why this garden was full of foxgloves.

He and his wife were constantly busy, manicuring their strange (and yet very ordinary) ill-sited garden, and polishing their house. He used to go about with a little hammer, tapping the stones, or labouring on his rockeries with pick and spade. I never found them sitting and enjoying their garden – pleasure was entirely in work and duty, and in pretending that the roof was not about to fall in. They totally ignored the fact that on wild winter nights we would often all hear a house or barn roof collapsing on the moor; and that the roofs of their house and of my cottage had deep sags, signifying rotten timbers. They had come here during the Second World War, escaping from Manchester and therefore in a position to claim that anyone who had survived Hitler's bombing was not going to be frightened by an old moorland farm falling in. One night, eventually, the roof of the little barn between our two houses did fall into the lane. The noise, heard from inside our bedroom, was cataclysmic, terrifying. I went out and met my neighbours inspecting it in the wind and the dark. Then we all went back to bed. The next day they tidied some of the fallen stones, talked of making the new space into a 'walled garden', and went back to tending unsuccessful azaleas, rhododendrons and tulips.

They were *comers-in*. Saddleworth has two terms for newcomers: 'foreigners', that is those who were born here, but whose ancestors were from elsewhere, and 'comers-in', that is, recent settlers.

When my neighbours arrived the supply of spring water was turned away from their house by an unwelcoming farmer. Cows were herded into the lanes and their droppings left to form a quagmire. But by the time I came to Saddleworth the comers-in had gained control and were pushing the prices up. For them the pubs demolished interior walls and filled up the new spaces with polystyrene fakes. The newsagents stocked *Vogue, She, The Observer* and *The Sunday Times*. For them the premises of the older industries were converted to sauna baths and art galleries. The old shops in the High Street changed hands and brightened into boutiques, restaurants, Do-It-Yourself shops and estate agents' offices. Because of them the quarry that had been slowly, for over a century, unveiling the view of Oldham that lay beyond the hill, found itself attacked in the local press as an 'eyesore'. For these people arts festivals were organised and the rough corners of the villages were given floral displays. Fashionable women idled in their homes, or amongst boutiques and tea-shops. The Further Education Institute flourished with classes on cake-decorating, flower-arranging, dog-training, pottery, holiday-makers' Spanish, art, and with my own 'creative writing'.

Not many of the original villagers made a profit out of this. They were inarticulate, educated to fear such places as doctors' surgeries, headmasters' waiting-rooms and lawyers' offices. They did not know what 'environment' and 'comprehensive education' and 'élitism' meant. They had not learnt the modern techniques of 'protest', nor to form groups in genteel fashion, through coffee mornings, Tupperware parties and meetings after the keep-fit class. So the typical traditional villager, who should be heir to his own place, found himself unable to affect public decisions. The men went into the factories, mostly in Oldham and the other nearby towns, early in the mornings, and returned home inept for anything but the most somnambulant television or desultory conversations in the pubs. Their women were similarly hidden away in the mills, or carrying buckets around the farms. They were never amongst the decision-makers behind social events but were always the servants who brewed tea and buttered bread.

Past generations of Saddleworth people once had great vigour and took a militant part in social change. Delph was a village that refused to accept the defeat of Radicalism even after the Peterloo Massacre, and continued to prepare for revolution with scythes and sharpened sickles hidden in barns and mill-lofts. It was a woman from Saddleworth, Annie Kenney, who with Christabel Pankhurst began the Suffragette Movement by protesting for votes for women at a Manchester election meeting in 1905. The shelves of local history books in Saddleworth Library show the will to participate in culture, to produce belles-lettres. Each valley has its still-revered poet; Tim Bobbin (an eighteenth-century schoolmaster-weaver-poet, who used dialect language with some of the elasticity and flamboyance of a James Joyce), Sam Bamford, and Saddleworth's Ammon Wrigley. It was a Saddleworth weaver, John o'Grinfilt (John of Greenfield) who wrote a nineteenth-century poem of chilling, terrible pathos:

Awm a poor cotton weaver, as mony a one knows,
Aw've nowt t'ate in the house, and aw've wore out me clothes,
You'd hardly give sixpence for all aw've got on,
Me clogs are worn out, an' stockings aw've none;
You'd think it were hard, to be sent into th'world
To clem* and do best as you can. . .

John o' Grinfilt's ballad, from the time of the Napoleonic Wars, was sung in Saddleworth pubs – where it had not been taught by 'folk-singers' but had survived through its own tradition. We had an Ammon Wrigley Society that held hot-pot 'suppers' in the Church Inn, where the landlord was able to recite verse after verse from Wrigley.

There was a conflict, now evident in every West Yorkshire village, between gentility and tradition; of tradition mocked by the glitter of gentility. And I saw Saddleworth, especially, as a place of conflicts even deeper than this one: conflicts that were the product of violent weather over the denuded uplands as much as of social forces, and which were expressed, from time to time, in murders.

Around Saddleworth church is a tangled graveyard with a monument to two people killed in the 'Bills o' Jacks murder'. At the end of the nineteenth century a father and his son were cut to pieces with an axe at an isolated pub which they kept on the road from Greenfield to Holmfirth. The murder, a famous newspaper story of the time, was never solved. Various people were accused, the most colourful being the 'platters': part-gypsies, part-tramps, who lived in makeshift shelters on the moors and earned a living by weaving rush baskets. The platters claimed rights to various patches of rushes, and it was thought that there'd been a quarrel over this.

And almost everyone knows about the notorious 'Moors Murders', in which Brady and Hindley buried the bodies of children on that moor at the back of the house in which we lived. It seemed to me that it was a symptom of the place itself that there took place in it the 'Bills o' Jack murder' and a series of the most sickening murders in our history.

Conflict is a continuous, defining feature of Yorkshire. It is the knowledge that their culture has been bitterly fought for that makes certain old people guard their inheritance. Conflict with the weather, with the steep gradients, with the shallow soil, was an element of daily life; whilst cheerfulness was a victory gained in harsh surroundings where few flowers grew.

Whilst I lived in Saddleworth I thought of art as having much to do with endurance. It was a philosophy that had more to do with my reflecting the environment, than with thinking about art. It seemed to me that to construct lines of poetry was to refine the understanding so that it could not be blunted by experience. In the art of the past I

* starve

114

was excited by the theme of the fight to survive and grow, in opposition to the somnambulant things that one is encouraged, or compelled, to think. I was moved by the pathos and the loneliness of that endurance. I admired in people who were not artists the ways they found to maintain their individual preferences, instincts, and even prejudices; and also the individual sense of rightness, which might be deeply buried and difficult to quarry, but which produces that stubborn resistance.

II

The stream that trickles out of the soaked Saddleworth peat, and down the crannies in the rocks that it washes so that they gleam with a tiny diamond or two of their native gold, is called the River Tame. It quickly gathers enough water to be worth calling a river. Its valley broadens to contain, like the Calder Valley, a dependency of industrial towns, and thus it flows through Mosley, Stalybridge, Dukinfield, Hyde and Stockport before joining the other small rivers that make up the great River Mersey. All are cotton towns; whilst northwards, continuing the loop made by the river, are Middleton, Rochdale and Oldham. The whole landscape is a basin filled at the end of the eighteenth and the first part of the nineteenth centuries by Irish immigrants, demobilised soldiers and dispossessed agricultural workers come to learn to weave.

In Cheshire, when harvesting the corn, they used to cut a track around the perimeter of the field and gradually approach the centre. Thus they drove the 'vermin' to the last remaining square yards of cover. Then as many men and boys as could be found stood around the edges with guns or sticks. Only then were the last few square yards cut, compelling the rabbits and hares to dash across the stubble and be easily slaughtered.

Intake Farm stood on the edge of Hyde, Ashton-under-Lyne, and Stalybridge, and was called 'Intake' because it had been a patch of land carved out of the open moor, but was now caught within one of the tightening claws of those industrial towns. It was like one of those oases of standing corn. Tommy Toat, who farmed it, was like one of those wild creatures waiting for the pincers to close, for his way of life to be snuffed out. His attitudes, his wariness, his separateness from other people, made him similar to the animals. He was a tiny, witty, intelligent man who could barely read and write because in childhood either snow or harvest-time had kept him from school. But he seemed to lack nothing in being illiterate, nor in never going away from Intake Farm; he never took a holiday, and called seaside towns 'a good advertisement for concrete'.

I knew him well because for five years I rented the labourer's cottage attached to his farm. The low grey building was half sunk into the earth as if it had grown within a wave of grasslands rather than been erected upon them. All its bulging extensions seemed to have grown organically, and I imagined that at different moments in its 400-year-history someone with nothing to do on a summer's day had gone out and built a bit more of it, wherever his fancy prompted. The house had risen into its shapes during the summer days as dough rises into a loaf in a warm oven.

At that time I earned a living by gardening at suburban houses and by teaching 'rural studies' in a place ironically called 'Flowery Field'. The soil of the school garden was half composed of cinders and grew very little other than the willow herb and chick-weed that naturally takes over the sites of ruined buildings and industrial tips. It lay under the fumes of a nearby factory that processed engine oil and sometimes they were so bad that they forced me back into the classroom. Like most young teachers I approached my work as if it was a crusade, and I wanted to give my pupils a sense of what the natural world meant to me; however, the really significant part of my life was lived in the evening and at weekends in my cottage at Intake Farm and in my own quarter-acre garden there.

The sixty acres of the farm seemed, to the casual visitor, almost entirely neglected. Because Tommy never used weed-killers or ploughed for re-seeding, his meadows were noticeable from the far side of the valley as brilliant splashes of yellow dandelions or of white daisies. They were my delight. The farm, with its close-hugging nest of sheds, carts, middens, and piles of timber that he brought in from demolition sites (he was saving them for 'fencing spars', though he was notorious for his ill-kept fences), seemed to be like some back-wash of jetsam cast upon the fields.

The paving stones of the lane had sunk at jagged angles so that it was difficult to sweep them after the herd of cattle that tramped by twice a day, and neither Tommy nor his wife Maggie found much time to clean the lane, anyway. One huge flat stone lying before his door (there was only one door to the house) was bright from Maggie's scrubbing, but you could not reach it without wearing wellington boots to wade through the mud and cow-flops. His hedges were neglected for years and it did not occur to him that the time spent laying and cutting them would easily be made up by not having to spend days looking for strayed cattle. Intake Farm was the one place where blackberry bushes thickened the hedges. They flowed down the banks and into the fields, with large gaps that were closed with a loose strand of wire some time after the cattle had strayed, if Tommy remembered to mend them at all.

These gaps, and the air of neglect, encouraged trespassers. His fields were crossed by vague footpaths, once the routes to mills, and if someone strayed from them across Tommy's grassland, and he knew of it because the dog barked or because Maggie (who never rested during the day) alerted him, it was one of the few things that would disturb his afternoon sleep. 'Get off there! That's our living you's trampling on! 'ave you no respect for folks' livelihood?'

In his faded working clothes stiffened with dried dung, he himself looked like a large cow-flop. He was thought of as lazy because every afternoon except during the hay-making season he slept in front of the kitchen stove, perhaps warming his feet by stretching them into the oven. Yet he was irrationally dedicated to the things that he loved.

On the farm there was no electricity, no gas, and the water came from a spring. His interest in mechanical inventions had stopped in about 1935. There was an eccentric pump to bring water from the spring to the shippen (cowhouse), an old haycutting machine that was like a spastic grasshopper, and a petrol motor to drive a milking machine that rarely worked, and which he didn't wish to use, anyway. He could easily, with grants, have obtained improvements to all these things, but he didn't want them. What he did love was his horses, and he kept two of them expensively and well, though he had little work for them. He liked to milk his cows primitively; and to electric light he preferred the ritual of lighting oil lamps.

He appreciated that it was a beautiful ritual. First he had to heat the gauze of the mantle by burning methylated spirit soaked into a padding held in a metal clip to the stem of the lamp. This lasted a few minutes whilst the blue flame died down and the gauze whitened with heat. Then he slowly pumped to build up the pressure of the paraffin fumes – if he pumped too hard the mantle burst into flames – so that gradually more and more light was given out, awakening in a dark room like a flower opening.

Though Tommy neglected so much, to the things that he cared for he gave that attention, that careful, joyous engrossment, working with delight at whatever pace they demanded, which is the craftsman's and the good artisan's secret. He kept pigs because he could make money more easily from them than from any other stock, but he disliked them and so they were left uncleaned for weeks in the collapsing sheds and old railway waggons around his farm. But his two horses were stabled in solid stone stables that were as clean as hospitals, decorated with fading prize-tickets from agricultural shows. His way of disregarding jobs that ought to be done, but were not urgent, for the sake of giving his attention to whatever captivated him at the moment, was childish and exasperating, particularly to Maggie, for whom he was always calling to support him in the variety of activities that filled his day. With the squawking of hens, grunting of pigs and the groan of cattle, 'Maggie! Maggie! Maggie!' was a regular farmyard noise, when he 'needed' her to hold a post that he was driving into the ground, to run back and forth with screws, hammer and spanner when he 'mended' the drinking bowls for the cattle in the shippen, or to help drive the pigs from one pen to another.

But this childishness, which matched his small size, was perhaps why neighbouring farmers indulged him when he was a nuisance to them – as he often was, with his cattle straying across their land, his fields and hedgerows perpetrating clouds of weed-seeds that drifted across their pastures – or why they didn't despise him for his bad farming practices. Amiably they nicknamed him 'Rancher'.

But sometimes at an auction a farmer would get is own back. 'I've just the beast for you, Tommy lad,' someone would whisper. 'Just your price.' Tommy could tell a good cow from a bad one better than most, but couldn't resist cheapness or the challenge of proving that he could turn a sickly beast into a plump one (which he often did, though sometimes his bargains died, or were hastily sold for meat for zoo animals).

In dry summer weather he was busy taking drums of water to cattle in the pastures. In winter he was shovelling snow so that he could get his milk to the end of the lane.

Mr Jim Stott, farmer, Mill Bank.

Throughout any day of the year his tendency for childish dispersal of his energies was anchored by one or two such unavoidable demands. Maggie rose some time before him (though they both got up a little later than most farmers do). He had to take the milk to the lane-end by nine-thirty, so he gulped a large mug of tea, and went out to the shippen. Delivering his milk was the only thing that made him take notice of time, and compelled him to keep a clock, a scratched and unpolished heirloom of a grandfather clock ticking always twenty minutes fast in a dark corner of the hallway like a sinister visitor; and the clock was the only thing that made him use the radio, listening to time-signals so that he could set his chronometer twenty minutes fast.

Calling out to Maggie to do one job after another whilst he moved from the udders of one cow to those of the next, he had the churns filled by nine o'clock on most days. He spent twenty minutes harnessing his horse, loading the cart and crossing his fields to the public highway. Both rested when they returned – the horse in the best pasture, or in the stable, according to the weather, and Tommy, after a heavy breakfast, sleeping on a chair with his feet in the oven of the stove. Only Maggie worked at this time. A restless, energetic woman, she cleaned the empty churns in the dairy, which was a bitterly unpleasant job without an efficient water supply, and a painful one in winter. In the late morning Tommy made sporadic attempts at repairs around the farm whilst Maggie fed the hens (Tommy sturdily thought of tending hens as women's work) and cooked an always heavy midday meal, as well as she could with Tommy calling for her every few minutes. After dinner Maggie sometimes also rested a little, not by sleeping, but by 'doing something in the house'.

During the afternoon Tommy harnessed the horse for a chore that depended on which day of the week it was. On Monday he travelled the back doors of school kitchens, factory canteens, restaurants and greengrocers' shops to collect swill for his pigs. When he went out one realised how incongruous he was in the modern world. At the farm he seemed as timeless as plants and animals; a peasant farmer would never have looked very different to him and even his clothes looked like those in a Flemish genre painting. But when riding his cart in the street, amongst cars and smart people, he seemed utterly incongruous. On Wednesday he did his 'night soil' round. Many outlying farms and cottages did not have flush toilets and Tommy was paid by the Cleansing Department to empty the buckets. They were called 'night soil' buckets with reference to the time at which they were supposed to be emptied, but Tommy did it during the afternoon. (It was said of him that he once dropped his jacket into a bin of night soil. He rolled up his shirt sleeve and plunged his arm into the bin. 'Jacket's no good now,' he said, 'but I've got me sandwiches in the pocket!') On another afternoon he did errands for his trade in scrap metal, or he hauled another load of timbers from a demolished mill. At the end of the afternoon he hurriedly fed his pigs. It was usually late evening before he milked his cows again. At any rate it was rare for him not to do it by the light of a paraffin lamp. And once a month, after he'd finished the evening's milking, he put on a neat black suit and, without Maggie, went ballroom dancing. He wore wellington boots through the mud to the end of the lane and there he changed into dancing pumps, leaving his wellingtons under the milk churn stand until he returned in the early hours of the morning.

It was only during hay-making time that this routine was much varied, and then a fury overtook him. He was always the first farmer in the district to attempt hay-making – not because he didn't know as well as anyone else that an early spell of sunshine might suddenly give way to rain and ruin the cut grass, nor because he didn't realise that it was more economic to wait until the crop grew longer; it was simply that he was called by the joy of hay-making.

He was nevertheless always a little later in starting than he intended, because his hay machine, which a wiser man would have made sure was in working order well before hay-time, needed mending on the first sunny day that he thought about it, after it had been lying in the corner of a field all winter. He was sixty years old when I knew him, he had been working on farms ever since he could walk, yet he had never learnt to prepare for hay-making.

But once he began he was relentless. As his barn filled it was as if it was the fulfillment of his whole life. Milking the cattle was left until dark and it would often be two o'clock in the morning when he finished. Then he would feed the hens and the pigs, Maggie trotting behind him with the paraffin lamp. On many mornings at around 3 a.m. instead of taking a little sleep he would, if there was a moon or bright starlight, go into a new field that had to be cut and take advantage of the dew on the grass to scythe a way for his hay machine round the edge of the field. (You cannot use a scythe on dry grass.) Tommy neither smoked nor drank; this hay-making and the care of his horses were his drug and his intoxication.

Tommy was a tenant on this land which his family had farmed for generations. One day I found him leaning on his ash stick in the yard, looking a little lost, as he often did during his working day when he was wondering what job to do next. Tears were drifting from his red eyes, caused, he said, by the March wind. Then he told me that the owners of Intake Farm had sold it for building land.

For a few months he tried to carry on his work as usual, but gradually he and Maggie retreated more and more amongst their dark furnishings. At last they were moved out to a council house on their own fields. Until the day he left he came out for just an hour or two each day to repair door-latches, fences or bits of walls on property that was to be destroyed and that did not in any case belong to him. That winter he even manured his fields although they were to be built upon the following year, and the bulldozer-drivers laughed at his foolishness.

Cattle waggons used to enter his yard about once a month. (He was always anxious and unhappy when his stock went to market, even though that was his living. Also he hated the drivers because they carelessly grazed walls, the bark of trees, and knocked gate stumps.) Now they were coming every few days to rid him of his stock. The hens were sold as 'chickens' to the Pakistanis who had a restaurant in town, and who regularly travelled the countryside to buy poultry. His yard and buildings became barren and empty and all that he could do by way of mothering his loved farm was to scrub out the buildings and the stones of his yard (in a way he had never found time to scrub them before), though now there was only dust instead of the regular droppings of cattle.

A site office was erected in the paddock. Because the gate was too narrow for them, bulldozers ripped through a wall and half a dozen trees, churning the raw rough gap into mud so that they could park their site-clearing machinery in the yard.

Last of all, a vet took his dog behind the empty shippen and injected it. I went too, because the dog knew me and would follow me. Tommy stayed indoors, doubtless listening for a howl, for the last noise. There was silence.

It was the end of my quarter-of-an-acre Garden of Eden, too. The five years I spent there were the only period so far when I have experienced that delicious, close association with the earth, the weather, the seasons, the plants and other creatures, which comes from working the land to produce not profit but a minimal livelihood.

So, in ending my walk here I had found my way back to one of my roots; to the closest contact I have ever had with the things I most care about. My memories are of physical work that was idyllic because I was not employed by anyone, and because it was part of my happy emotions about the world that was around me. Of the joy of laying a thorn hedge, of rhythmically driving a post into the ground, of milking a cow, learning that a tender sensitivity must exist between man and beast if milk is to be drawn; of learning that there is a seasonal timing, that cannot be slowed or hurried, to the growth of plants.

There are memories of summer mornings before I went to teach at Flowery Field. Then I would go out to my garden as it came light, maybe at half-past five or at six o'clock, to hoe plants, mend a fence, collect eggs and clean out my hens, whilst I watched the stars extinguish and the grey, crepuscular light brighten, turn slowly fiery, and suddenly be overcome by the great throbbing ball of the sun. A little later I would hear our baby cry in the cottage, or I would know that my wife had risen when she lit the paraffin lamp and it throbbed like a heart, like the heart of the cottage itself, and then brightened as if it shouted in the room. I would see the light move into a lower room as she came downstairs; whilst on some days the sun would come so hot, even at six or seven o'clock in the morning, that I would take off my shirt, shoes and socks, and work.

The rhythm of the labour sent a glowing happiness through my limbs. And through working regularly in a physical way I learnt to be more tender in my handling of things. It is quite impossible to handle spade, hoe, axe, spanner or scythe for more than an hour or two without getting crippling pains, unless you discover and enter into a natural rhythm dictated by the tool. Perhaps it taught me to be more tender and craftsman-like with words.

Having discovered these rhythms of work, and this exquisite, gentle association with the world, it seemed that to be impatient, to tear its symphonies of quiet sounds and movements, of birds, animals, plants and tools with impatient gestures, to poison the land and its creatures with weed-killers and insect-poisons, or excessively and brutally to formalise the land, or to treat my own person crudely, to drink, smoke, or to eat excessively, was to profane some marvellous source of joy. Every natural thing was numinous, and I would lose the sense of this if I did anything excessive.

And, I am convinced, it was something like these feelings that directed Tommy Toat, despite his fecklessness, his wayward scruffiness, to cling to his way of life.

The extinction of Tommy Toat – and with it the extinction of my own way of life, which I have found so difficult to return to since – was part of the reckless destruction of an unassessed and disregarded culture, being relentlessly destroyed here, just as it is in most places now.

There is a much-used phrase that describes the loss of hold upon the land. 'The moor's coming closer down every year,' the old people say when they see what were patches of green cultivated field on the sides of the moor turning brown through neglect. But here and there, long after the farmer has left and his house has been taken over by someone not interested in the land, you see patches of brighter green unusually high up the moor. They were pastures that were so well cared-for that the moor still finds it difficult to encroach upon them with its brown rushes and sour, dead grey grass. Intake Farm shows in that way. And on its slightly brighter grass a certain consciousness was born in me.

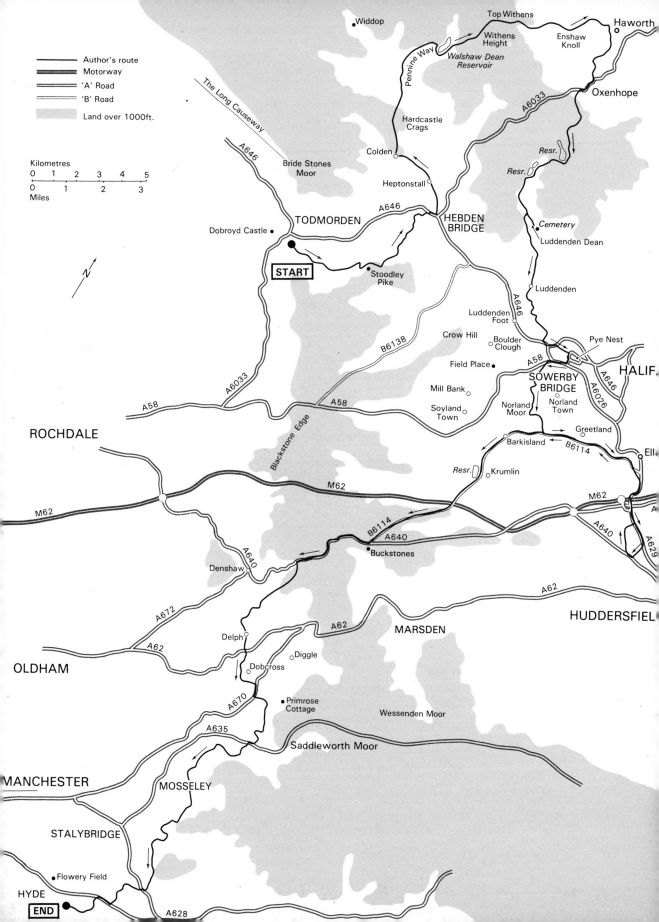